The Zen of Blogging

MAKE MONEY WITH YOUR BLOG, FIRE YOUR BOSS AND LIVE THE GOOD LIFE.

By Daniel Welsch
Copyright © Daniel Welsch, 2017
More on the web: expatmadrid.com/book
Cover Design by Krish Designz.
Cover Illustration: karpenko_ilia / Shutterstock.

Table of Contents

Warning 7
Now and then 9
While we're here 11

PART 1: NUTS AND BOLTS
My first winter in Madrid 15
My life as a writer and as a failure 18
How to start a blog 34
Massive Action and Tiny Excuses 43
Sturgeon's Law 47
Logos, design, and themes for your blog 55
How to monetize your blog 59
Tools, tips and tricks 68
SEO and Getting Traffic 72
Social Media 74
Email marketing 75

PART 2: THE BLOGGER LIFESTYLE
A day in the life of a (semi) professional blogger 79
Chop wood, carry water 85
Good writing habits 87
5 things I've been asking myself since becoming
a professional blogger 90
How to become an influencer on Instagram 97
Warning: You probably don't want to be
a digital nomad 103
A day in the life: London Edition 110
High Quality Problems 118
Epilogue 120
And by the way... 122
Thank You 123

Warning

• • • •

This isn't your typical feelgood how to book.

You can definitely earn money as a blogger, and I'm living proof. But it isn't always easy. It takes work, time, and a dedication to learning.

Also, you gotta be willing to step out of your comfort zone.

That voice in your head that makes excuses about why you can't do things?

Kill it.

It's not gonna get you where you want to go.

In this book you'll learn how to start a blog, how to start making money, and basically everything I know that's helped me fire my boss, become location independent, double my income and then double it again.

Everything that's helped me live with no rules, no set schedule, no day job, and no alarm – the only time I set an alarm these days is when I've got an early flight to somewhere awesome.

So here's the warning...

It's not all pretty rah-rah stuff.

If you're going to be a pro blogger, a digital nomad, a lifestyle designer or whatever you want to call it, you've gotta do what other people won't.

But hey, that's the same for anything. Wanna be a world-class ping pong player? Well guess what... you've gotta do what other people won't.

Just get used to it.

Being normal isn't paying a lot of dividends.

When you have an online business, you're you've gotta solve problems that would leave lesser mortals crying into their pillow and giving up. And don't get me wrong: I've cried into my pillow a couple times during these years.

But then I got up, dusted it off, and got back to work. That's the key.

And in the end it's all worth it, because I've had some amazing experiences, met some great people, earned more money than I ever thought I would, and travelled all over Europe on the proceeds.

And guess what... it all started that first time I hit "publish".

Ready for all the juice?

Here goes...

Now and then

••••

I dropped out of college when I was 19.

It wasn't doing much for me.

All I wanted to do in life was travel around, have adventures, and write about them.

And being an English major seemed like a long, slow path towards slinging cappuccinos at my local Starbucks... while also getting into tens of thousands of dollars of debt.

I figured I could skip the debt and go straight to Starbucks.

So I dropped out.

And Starbucks didn't hire me.

Incidentally, neither did McDonald's.

When I think back on embarrassing moments in my life, driving my broken-down pickup to McDonald's to drop off an application, and then going home to wait for a call that never came is pretty high on the list.

But looking back, everything else that happened came from that rejection.

I got a job at a smaller local coffee shop, and I was known by at least two or three people as making the best cappuccino in the area north of Phoenix.

Nobody ever said that about Lord Byron.

If I had gotten the job at McDonald's, by now I might be manager... Lording it over a half dozen fry cooks on the southwest corner of two roads to nowhere in middle of the Arizona desert.

I'd have moved up to a reasonably priced Japanese car, and I'd spend 60 hours a week wearing a regulation polo shirt that smelled like stale grease and pink slime.

Instead, I moved to Spain and became a professional blogger.

Okay, okay... hang on.

It wasn't quite as easy as that.

I had to bust my ass in low paying jobs for years, and blog all the while as an escape plan.

But two years ago, when I finally fired my boss and walked off into the sunset...Well... let's just say it was **fucking epic**.

And now, here I am. Blogging happily ever after.

And guess what... Remember rebellious little dropout Daniel, who only wanted to travel around, have adventures, and write about them?

Well, he'd probably think the guy I've become now is kind of a douche. Way too confident, too loud, too smiley.

But he got everything he wanted.

Travel across many countries, freedom from meaningless wage-slavery, fun, adventure, excitement... and lots of opportunities to write about it.

What rebellious little dropout Daniel really wanted – back in the distant year we called 2002 – was to play by his own rules. To answer to nobody. To live outside "normal" society. To do something actually meaningful with his life. Something he cared about.

Most of all, he wanted something better than to rot in a cubicle from Monday through Friday, stomach churning with dread, student loan bills or mortgage payment due on the first.

And he got it. He got every last one of his goddamn unreasonable teenage demands.

Here's how...

While we're here

• • • •

Before we get into the meat of the book, check out my website expatmadrid.com/book

Go sign up for my emails and I'll send you new ideas, tips, tricks, resources you love and much much more.

It'll be worth your while, I promise.

And of course, you can unsubscribe whenever you want. (More about email marketing later on. It's the key to almost everything.)

····· PART ONE ·····

Nuts and Bolts

Everything you need to know to get started and make your blog great.

Part 1: Nuts and Bolts

My first winter in Madrid

I first came to Spain in summer, on vacation. And few months later, I came back for love.

Or at least for a girl.

The details aren't too important. I was sitting on the edge of a fountain in Granada and she came up to say hi. We were travelling on the same basic route, so a few days later we met up in Madrid, where she was studying.

In total, we spent a couple of days and nights together, and by the time I got back to Phoenix, things just didn't seem the same.

So I put my affairs in order and hopped on another plane. All that tip money from slinging cappuccinos added up to enough to live on for a few months… Madrid was cheap, and I was used to living on next to nothing in the US.

Everything was going fine, until the dollar collapsed. It just couldn't keep up with the strong euro in those pre-crisis days. In my first few months abroad, I saw about a third of my savings disappear into the exchange rate void.

No matter.

I didn't have any idea what I was doing anyway. And actually, I was kind of expecting to die young like my favorite rock stars or Romantic poets.

There was no five-year plan. No vision. No mission statement.

If you'd told me, back in '04, that I should read *The 7 Habits of Highly Effective People,* I would've spit in your eye.

Now it's one of my favorite books. But that was then.

Part 1: Nuts and Bolts

Then, it was more like "Let's go have an adventure in Europe, see what happens. Meet some cute girls, see some nice architecture, die young far from home."

Sounds stupid and lame, doesn't it? But hey. I was 21. And in the end it seems to have worked out pretty well.

I arrived in Madrid on a Thursday morning, and called Elsa. She told me to meet her on a plaza in her neighborhood.

When I got there, 28 metro stops later, it was a cold day in late October, and there was a persistent drizzle falling on me, my backpack, and my duffel bag. This was everything I now owned.

Elsa was late, I was getting cold, and as I looked around I realized: this plaza was pretty dismal and grey.

I started to wonder if I was making a big mistake.

From there, that winter just got colder.

I found a room to rent, a couple of metro stops from Elsa's place. The neighborhood was bad. Half the houses seemed to be squatted, cars would burn in the middle of the night leaving charred skeletons I would find on my walk to the Metro in the morning. There was a fat guy who'd walk around the park in the evenings, shooting at pigeons with a pellet gun.

Of course, I was just astounded to be in Europe. Multi-story buildings, a walkable neighborhood with cafés, shops and transport... it was my lifelong dream! To walk out of the house and be somewhere. I only figured out how bad that first neighborhood was much later, after moving on to another.

In the meantime, I stumbled into English teaching. Originally, I'd wanted to avoid it – as a painfully shy kid with no social skills, I'd figured I'd hate teaching.

I was wrong.

Once I'd decided it was the only reasonable way for me to make a living in Spain, it took me about four days to find a job.

Part 1: Nuts and Bolts

And after doing a few classes, I was shocked to find that a badly-paid job could be so much fun.

Time passed, as time always does. I started to settle into another rut. Better than the one back home, but still... A rut is a rut.

From that winter, what I remember most is this: It's around midnight, and I'm sitting alone on the bed in my tiny rented room, clutching a mug of hot tea, hands numb from the cold.

And suddenly, I have a revelation. Looking back, it seems a bit obvious.

What I realized was: this was all my fault.

Nobody else was to blame for my life up to now. Nobody had encouraged me to drop out of school or to move halfway across the world for a girl I barely knew.

I had gone against the recommendations of lots of "responsible" adults to get here. I had refused all sorts of reasonable advice.

Go back to school, do something useful with myself, see a psychologist.

All reasonable, adult courses of action that I'd ignored.

And now, if I was going to make something of my life, it was going to be entirely on me.

Nobody else was going to walk into this cold-ass room in the worst neighborhood of Madrid to solve my problems for me.

So I'd better get to work solving them myself.

And I did.

Nothing was the same after that night.

Part 1: Nuts and Bolts

My life as a writer and as a failure

Stephen King says, about life as a writer:

"Amateurs sit and wait for inspiration, the rest of us just get up and go to work."

Don't I know it.

Recently I celebrated my 7th year of blogging – and I'm coming up on 2 years in which I make a full-time living from my blogs, books and online courses.

There is **one basic key** to writing that I know of: you've just gotta sit down and do it.

Pound that keyboard a few hours a day and you're a writer.

Don't, and you're not.

There's no productivity trick or mobile app that will save you from actually doing the work.

And while we're here: **fuck inspiration.**

Or at the very least, let me tell you: inspiration is overrated. And most of the time it comes while you're already in the middle of writing.

Anyway...

7 years as a blogger, 2 years as a full time pro.

I've learned a lot in this time. Mostly, it must be said, from failure.

And I'm going to tell you all about it.

So read on...

Part 1: Nuts and Bolts

Humble beginnings at Kinko's

Back in Phoenix, I used to write zines.

Laid out by hand and photocopied – I'd stuff my backpack with hundreds of copies, and walk up to the register with a few dozen sheets in my hand.

"Just these, thanks!"

Can't knock the hustle.

The first zine I wrote was about cycling as a political statement.

It sold a couple hundred copies through various distributors at $2 each, and I felt pretty successful as a writer.

The next ones all flopped, mostly because I tried to write about my daily life.

Portland dominated zine culture in the early 2000s, and if you were from Portland, you could write about your bus trip across the state or your crush on the vegan barista or your critique of consumer society.

If you were from Phoenix, apparently nobody cared.

Oh well.

I got used to the rejections from tattooed hipsters from places I'd never visited.

And soon I was on my way to Spain, and my career in zines came to an end…

Teenage angst hasn't paid off well

A year or so after moving abroad, once I was settled in, I started to write a novel about my teen angst.

The story was told from 5 different points of view (inspired by Faulkner, if I recall) and included fictionalized versions of basically everyone I knew back home.

Part 1: Nuts and Bolts

I never even tried to publish it.

I didn't care. (And I more than suspected that the world just didn't need to know about my teen angst.)

In any case, the process was reward enough – spending 6 or 8 months on a completely self-directed project was eye-opening. I was apparently capable of finishing big things.

This was the first sort of minor "achievement" I'd ever had in my life.

So why didn't I try to publish it?

Well, I knew something about getting published – it apparently involved long years of heartbreak and rejection. (Kind of like my love life, now that I think about it.)

I didn't want to go through that, with my fragile 23-year-old ego.

So I didn't.

That summer, I finished my second draft on a borrowed desktop computer in a borrowed room. My first full summer in Madrid.

Elsa had gone back to her country to have a "real life" and I spent that summer dating a tiny, dark-haired actress. She was intense, beautiful, and possibly a pathological liar. I was hopelessly in love with her, in my sad 23-year-old way.

I know, I know...

When I said I moved halfway across the world for a girl, you were probably hoping for some story of endless monogamy – the fun kind that exists only in our unreasonable Disney fantasies.

Didn't happen.

Sorry.

When I finished the second draft of my novel and put a copy away for safekeeping, I was pretty exhausted with writing.

Part 1: Nuts and Bolts

Then the tiny dark-haired actress dumped me, and I had a sort of crisis of meaning.

I gave up on literature and took up boxing. Punching people in the face, getting knocked down and getting back up to punch them again – that was real. Much healthier than living in my head all day, making up stories.

After that, it took me years to start writing again.

This time as a blogger...

Creating my media empire, a post at a time

Several years passed. Not much happened, but at the same time a lot happened.

You only get to be young once. And I guess I enjoyed it quite a bit, despite being broke and an illegal immigrant.

I was working 6 days a week, from 8 AM to 10 PM, giving English classes to everyone from teenagers to tycoons.

The schedule was the worst part. From early morning to late night I might only have 5 or 6 hours of work. Then I'd have 4 hours of transport, and the rest was dead time to sit in a park or read on a bench. Rarely enough to go home for a nap, although that was what I most needed.

I learned a lot of Spanish reading newspapers and cheap paperbacks on buses. I managed to save enough to get through another summer, and then another. I moved through a series of shared flats.

I keep track of the chronology of those years by remembering what girl I was dating.

If I was with Eve from Paris when it happened, it must have been 2008. If I was with the Bulgarian model, 2009.

(She wasn't really a model. She was just an idle rich girl who looked like one. Why she dated me, briefly, is something I'll never understand.)

Part 1: Nuts and Bolts

In the spring of 2010 I was with Laura, a feisty Italian, when a friend told me I should have a blog about English.

He was living at my place, and already making money online – I'd see him there on the sofa at all hours of the day and night, hunched over his laptop and swearing under his breath.

And some months, at least, he was able to pay the rent.

Seemed better than running around town all day giving classes.

We were sharing a flat in the south of Madrid – by now I had moved up to the second-worst neighborhood in the city.

And summer was just about to begin.

By now I had realized that at some point in June, all my income was going to dry up. People will talk all spring about how this summer they're really gonna knuckle down and learn English... but when they actually have to decide between spending the afternoon at the swimming pool or going to English class, they choose the pool.

And who can blame them?

I'd spend the time from July 1st to mid-October watching the contents of my "secret money sock" head towards zero... That first paycheck after the long Spanish summer was one of the best moments of my year.

So despite having no idea what I was doing, I started madridingles.es soon after my friend's recommendation.

My first idea was to start the blog, get some business cards printed up, and jack up the prices of my private lessons...

Based solely on the prestige that "having a website" gives you.

It didn't work.

For one thing, the Spanish economy had already started its long, slow collapse.

Part 1: Nuts and Bolts

That made people much more price conscious.

And when I actually did the math, even charging 35€ an hour for private lessons wouldn't change my life too much – if I still had to go across town on the metro to get there.

45 minutes there, 45 minutes back, all for an hour of class... the numbers didn't work out.

Even in the best case, I'd only be able to work 20 hours a week. And even that was a stretch.

I decided to change tactics.

My tech knowledge was still hovering near zero, but soon, my humble blog was covered with ugly ads for language schools and miracle weight loss methods.

That didn't work either. I did the math a few months in, and realized I'd need about half a million pageviews a month to make ends meet that way.

So I did something different.

Key lesson: don't be afraid to change direction.

All that led me to...

My first Kindle book

One day a guy on an online forum mentioned he had just published a book on Amazon.

I was a bit puzzled, because he seemed to be just another guy with an internet connection – a guy just like me, only in England.

Googling around, I learned that anybody could publish a Kindle book.

So I did.

Key lessons here: 1) Google is your friend. 2) Take action. Now, goddammit!

Part 1: Nuts and Bolts

For a couple of weeks in July 2012, I wrote my first ebook. It was about phrasal verbs. You know – those expressions like get up, wake up, break up and break down that you've been using your whole life without thinking about them.

People from other countries find them endlessly frustrating, and I had been teaching them in class for years. I figured there might be a market.

Anyway, my flatmates were out of town, which meant that I could sit at the kitchen table in my boxer shorts all afternoon, sweating and struggling with the first draft.

We had an air conditioner, but couldn't afford to use it.

Did I mention I was living in Spain illegally?

Yeah, that too.

When I arrived, my whole plan was "overstay my tourist visa and figure it out later". Which eventually, I did.

But at the time, it sucked.

In any case, I had some ambition.

My (then) girlfriend was, as I mentioned, Italian – so of course she was a graphic designer. I got her to make a basic book cover, uploaded everything to the Kindle site, and bam!

I was a published author.

It sold a few copies almost immediately, mostly to readers of my blog. And kept selling a couple of copies every week.

Two or three months later I was in a private class with an executive working in marketing. He was like that cool uncle and I was the scruffy rebellious nephew with no life plan. We got on swimmingly.

That day in class, I mentioned my "success" on Amazon – dozens and dozens sold! – and he gave me what is probably the best advice I'd ever gotten from a mature adult.

"Daniel", he said, "You've found the thing that's going to make you rich. Now work harder!"

Thanks, man.

I'm not rich yet. But I'm certainly working harder.

Another key lesson: Writing can be lonely. Get support from others.

Actually, I can trace most of my success as a blogger to basically two things...

One, I picked a topic that people were already interested in and spending money on.

Two, I got encouragement almost immediately from a couple of random strangers. Besides, the executive, a girl I barely knew named Sara shared everything I did on Facebook, and a guy from Venezuela named Renzo started sending me questions to answer on the blog.

It made me feel like somebody. And like I was doing something important. I had an audience, more or less from the beginning.

An audience of two or three is still an audience. If people are interested, you've got proof of concept.

And that was all I needed to get through those first couple of months where most bloggers give up.

I wasn't finished failing yet, though...

My next book completely bombed. I think I sold 5 copies – at least 2 of them to friends.

Looking back, it's perfectly clear why: no message to market match.

It was about **teaching** English, and my whole audience was **learning** English.

They didn't care.

Part 1: Nuts and Bolts

Key lesson: nobody's gonna buy a book just 'cause you took the time to write it. What's in it for them?

The funny thing is that while I was writing that book, I was already convinced of my own genius.

A book about teaching English in Spain!

I was going to the top with this one... It was a great idea. Obviously. All my friends were English teachers in Spain, so clearly there was a market.

How could I fail?

How indeed.

My third book was conceived at an Italian airport – Bologna, perhaps – just after Christmas, while my flight was delayed.

Laura was there, and she was pissed.

Italian-style pissed.

Don't ask.

So I used writing as a convenient excuse to ignore her for a couple of hours. I came up with a frantic sort of outline there in the airport and got to work the next morning, back in Madrid.

By this time I was no longer convinced of my own genius, but figured I'd keep trying things anyway.

Throw enough shit at the wall and some of it would stick.

I wrote the third one mostly for myself... with low expectations. I just wanted to get all that "language learning theory" out of my head so I could continue with my life.

I published it, and for several months sales were slow. I sold a few dozen copies, like I had with my first book.

But that summer, back in Italy, I was so bored I got out my prehistoric smartphone and managed to connect to the internet long enough to find that I was somehow **#1 in the education category** on Amazon.

Part 1: Nuts and Bolts

I'm not sure what happened.

But suddenly I was on my way to the top again.

Back in Madrid that autumn, I did some very optimistic calculations (what if this 400% monthly growth continues forever?) and then wrote an email to my marketing guru in the US, telling him I hoped to soon be joining his $25,000 a year coaching program.

LMFAO.

I did spend some time at #1 and #2 in the education and language learning categories.

But I didn't suddenly become a big fish and get to hang out at events with Tony Robbins.

Either way, I now had a solution to all my financial problems: **write more $4 ebooks**.

How could I fail?

How indeed.

Dominating the interwebs, firing my boss…

I started getting a lot more traffic on the blog.

And I wrote a few more books. I can still remember with giddiness the day I sold a book in the first hour after launch – and 3 copies on the first day.

"C-notes by the layers, true fuckin' players", as Biggie said.

I made something like 8 dollars that launch day, and I was bubbling with happiness.

My income as a writer was slowly improving, month by month… And after another year, it was good enough to be able to afford to beer and cheap cuts of meat all summer long – my friends were eating rice and drinking water, so this was clearly a step up.

Having a few c-notes to rub together is great for a young guy's self-esteem, too. Especially if he was expecting to be scraping along near the bottom of society forever.

The second-best moment of my writing life (up to now) was when I was able to quit one of my part-time jobs – the one that was making me most miserable.

Just to be evil, I wrote my resignation email to the Director of Studies on a Monday an hour before I was due to be in class.

Then ignored him as he proceeded to blow up my phone.

I didn't need him.

Bitch, please. I'm a writer now.

In the meantime, I had published a very unsuccessful book about business English, and failed at wine blogging.

When I started the wine blog, I imagined cases upon cases of free wine arriving at my door, as I gained prestige in the oenosphere. I had probably heard about Gary Vaynerchuk by that point and figured I'd emulate him.

Or maybe I hadn't.

Either way, I soon gave up on that one.

I could – and someday will – write about the debauchery that is likely to result from the combination of me, a willing female and a cold bottle of sherry on a hot summer day.

But it turns out I didn't have shit to say about wine.

Fruity. Oaky. Who cares?

I just wanna drink it.

Key lesson: write about something you care about. Don't get into it just because you think you'll earn money or get free stuff.

Get rich slowly…

Ok, ok, I'm still not rich.

But I'm making a living as a pro blogger – something very few people ever manage to do.

Eventually I figured out that it was going to be very slow and very painful getting rich a few bucks at a time.

I just wasn't going to retire on Kindle ebook sales.

It was time to raise prices.

So I made a couple of online courses for Gumroad, then for Udemy. I already had a market: several people had told me "Daniel, if you make an online course, I'll buy it".

I didn't know anything about online courses, and it seemed like a lot of work. But it's hard to resist an offer like that.

Still, the first few times I sent out an email asking people to spend $17 were absolutely terrifying. After that, $27 was terrifying. Then $37.

Now I'm at $97 and lemme tell you something: every time I raise prices it's terrifying at first.

And every time I do it, my life immediately gets better.

Today, if I had a gun to my head and needed 10,000 bucks by the end of the week, I'd come up with some product or coaching program for $500, and just try to sell 20. Or maybe $5000 and just try to sell two of them.

And then I'd pray...

'Cause after we've already seen, I'm wrong as often as I'm right about these things.

My personal Victory in Europe

The best moment of my writing career so far was a day about two years ago when Amazon decided to promote one of my books at a 70% discount.

I bombed my email list with the offer and refreshed Amazon on my (now much smarter) phone every 10 minutes, all day long.

Part 1: Nuts and Bolts

Other than that, it was a long work day on a terrible salary. Buses and trains from class to class, starting before dawn and ending after dark.

At 6:30 in the evening, I finished my last class in some godawful suburb.

And at eight I had a date with a girl I thought was THE one.

At around 7:15 I was on the bus back to civilization, and Amazon updated the rankings. I was on top.

Not the education category.

No, no...

On top of all Amazon Spain.

I was ahead of Harry Potter, ahead of 50 Shades of Grey.

I was the #1 author in the whole goddamn country.

I could barely control myself.

When 8 o'clock came, I met, uh, let's call her Esther – and collapsed into her arms, an exhausted, euphoric mess.

"I'm #1", I whispered in her ear.

We kissed. Her lips were like roses.

For a few brief hours, I was the best selling writer in Spain. And happily in love as well. I took Esther to dinner, and we got tipsy on red wine and orujo.

I was as happy as I've ver been.

But the next day, I was up at 6:15 again, in order to be in class at 8 AM.

Physically I was there – mentally, I was done.

I decided I'd finish my contract. Do my classes till June 30.

And that was it.

No more wage slavery.

Part 1: Nuts and Bolts

I was going to declare victory over the European labor market. Victory over Spanish wages. Victory over all the shitty jobs on all the shitty schedules for all the shitty language academies.

Victory over all the bosses who treated me like I was nobody. Did any of them have a bestselling book?

No. None of them.

I changed my computer wallpaper to a photo of Winston Churchill – a man of action if there ever was one – giving the V for Victory during World War II.

It was time to make my own V.E. Day.

I made a plan, mentally committed myself to life as a full-time writer, and started the countdown to Victory in Europe.

11 weeks.

10 weeks.

So far so good.

Towards the end of week 9, Esther dumped me.

At the time I was so focused on my mission that I didn't care... much. It took me several months to realize exactly how much it was affecting me.

In the meantime, the countdown continued.

The school year ended, I cashed my severance check and went to the East of Europe to celebrate.

I was free. And kinda miserable.

Walking around Budapest, Esther's face still floated through my mind seven times an hour... I still wanted her. I still wished I could fall asleep next to her at nights and wake up with her in the mornings.

The nights we'd brushed our teeth together before bed haunted me with their feeling of love and quiet domesticity.

I wanted her back.

Part 1: Nuts and Bolts

And it just wasn't going to happen.

I caught a train to Zagreb. It left two hours late and took 4 hours longer than scheduled. It was full of British and Australian backpackers with broad shoulders and wifebeaters. The flower of youth, or something. Finally, after two changes of train and an awkward conversation with a border guard who had never heard of Madrid, I arrived in the Balkans.

Zagreb has something called the Museum of Broken Relationships. Of course I went. And of course I regretted it.

I decided to get drunk on palinka and try to pull Eastern European waitresses back to my AirBnB. It didn't work.

And soon I was back in Madrid, facing life with no structure, no schedule. Nothing but a lot of time to sit and think.

Key lesson: Success can solve financial problems. But a lot of the bigger problems aren't financial.

And two years later, my life as a writer continues...

I could write a whole book about the things that have happened during last two years.

For now, let's just say: running your own business is hard.

Now you know.

Personally, I had no idea. I had basically no role models to tell me how this all works. Among people in my social class back home, starting your own business was considered a form of insanity.

I was in uncharted territory.

Listen: I was expecting to retire. Write a few emails a week from the beach, and live on passive income. That's what the lifestyle designers claim they're doing.

How could I fail?

Part 1: Nuts and Bolts

How indeed.

So here's the thing: the internet's changing, and fast.

In these 2 years, among other things, the Spanish government killed my website (gotta love Europeans and their regulations) and Udemy, the online course platform where I was making all my money, changed their algorithm – which suddenly cut my revenue by 90%.

Oops.

I've learned a lot about planning and plan B-ing, about rolling with the punches, and about the futility of "passive income".

I've changed course a couple of times, and I'm doing better than ever. But it wasn't easy.

So I've failed at retirement...

But had quite a few adventures in the process.

Key lesson: the game doesn't end till you die.

As Stephen Pressfield says,

"Fear doesn't go away. The warrior and the artist live by the same code of necessity, which dictates that the battle must be fought anew every day."

I'm hardly an artist. Or a warrior. But that's one of my favorite quotes.

Now get out there and write, my loves.

Part 1: Nuts and Bolts

How to start a blog

So now I'm a professional blogger.

And there aren't very many of us.

I just know a couple of people like me, whose blog and related content is their main source of income.

Others use a blog to support their main business – to build their reputation as experts in their field. Which works fine... actually it was my original plan. Didn't work out for me. But hey.

Here we are.

(I'll be talking more about exactly how to monetize a blog later.)

In any case, let's get this out of the way at the beginning:

Writers are usually pretty badly paid. By which I mean that most writers earn next to nothing.

There are always the Kings, Pattersons, Rowlings and such who earn hundreds of millions over the course of their careers.

They make us all look bad. 'Cause most writers don't earn that much.

If you want to have some idea about the top dogs in the writing world, read Stephen King's On Writing. It won't tell you how to start a blog or make half a billy online, but it's certainly interesting and has some useful advice about style and storytelling – plus his life story is amazing.

In any case, you **can** earn money with a blog. Maybe a lot of money... depends on you, your topic, your audience, and lots of other factors.

But if I can do it, anyone can do it.

Part 1: Nuts and Bolts

You just have to be flexible and willing to put in the work.

Anyway...

As a professional blogger, I get questions all the time: How do I start a blog? How do I make money?

I'm going to take a stab at answering the most important questions about blogging here... so that in the future, I can just tell people to buy my book rather than giving them the whole speech.

(Time management is pretty important for anyone – especially the self-employed and entrepreneurial.)

So without further ado...

Here's my best advice about how to start a blog.

How to start a blog (and eventually make money)

Keep in mind, I'm just one guy and not nearly as rich as some other bloggers.

But at the same time, I've made it.

If your writing income is larger than your rent payment in any given month, you're basically an elite writer. That's just how publishing works.

And the blogosphere is similar, from what I've been able to figure out: a few people make a lot of money, a few more are able to earn a living, most earn very little or nothing.

I'm making a living, and it's enough to fund my lifestyle in Spain, my copious steak and wine consumption, and my travels around Europe.

I have enough left over to invest. But I'm no online bazillionaire.

So by all means... If you want some advice from the real experts, check out some people at the top as well. Many of them are willing to take you behind the scenes once in a while and it's quite interesting.

Anyway, without further ado...

Rule #1 – Just get started

I'm serious.

The world doesn't care about your business plan. The world doesn't care about your logo or your design or your domain name.

You will never make money off the blog you're "going to" write. I promise.

So just get started. Go to WordPress.com and set one up.

Now.

Or get a goddamn tumblr for all I care.

I spent 6 years on tumblr, made some money and built myself quite a reputation – and all because I didn't have the tech knowledge to start a "real blog".

And that's another thing...

Forget all your excuses.

'Cause you ain't gonna pay your rent with excuses either.

You don't need tech knowledge, a logo, a business plan, a Facebook page or anything else – yet. I know because I started out without all those things.

And here's the brutal truth: most people who say they want to start a blog will never do it. The rest won't make it to 10 posts before giving up.

There's a lot of competition among new bloggers in the blogosphere. But not many people who are actually putting in the work and playing the long game.

My first piece of advice to new bloggers, then, is the following:

Part 1: Nuts and Bolts

1. Get a piece of paper.
2. Make a list of 10 posts you could write about some topic you enjoy.
3. Open up a WordPress.
4. Sit down and write post #1.
5. Publish it.
6. Repeat steps 4 and 5 until you've gotten through the list (feel free to do this over a space of 5 to 10 days).
7. Evaluate what's gone well and what hasn't up till now.
8. Continue with idea generation and writing, potentially forever.

And that's about it. Incidentally, this is the same advice I got from a friend years ago. It's the advice that got me started. And look at me now.

So really, just start.

You ain't shit 'till you've actually published 10 posts.

(If you're offended by my use of colloquial English in this book, I respect that. But see Rule #3.)

Rule #2 – Think topic, think audience

Getting started is really the most important thing. You should have a general idea of the topic, but that will probably change with time.

If you keep blogging, **you'll** change.

You'll develop new interests, new ideas. You'll learn things you never imagined when you were starting out, and you'll have the unique and beautiful opportunity to take your audience along for the ride.

Part 1: Nuts and Bolts

You don't need a perfectly clear idea of your topic to start out, but make sure your general topic is something you're going to be into for the long haul.

Lifestyle design or digital nomads might be the fashionable thing now, but do you really want to write hundreds of posts about one or the other?

I don't.

Write about something you're truly interested in.

And by the way – just in case you're thinking you're going to start a blog about how to make money blogging, despite the fact that you've never actually made money blogging…

I've just got two syllables for you:

Fuck off.

And a third one:

Die.

Anyway…

All this talk about your topic is useless, of course, unless you also have an idea of who your audience will be.

Mostly, think about this: **does your topic actually have an audience?**

The internet is great because it's a place where the few weirdos are interested in one-legged midget boxing or *Twilight* fan fiction can get together. Those people who might, a couple of decades ago, have died alone without ever meeting anyone sharing their bizarre interests.

But not every topic is necessarily interesting to a large enough audience to make it profitable or otherwise worth your time.

If you want to blog about your personal drama with your friends, or about your fetish for stuffing your underwear with origami owls, go right ahead…

Part 1: Nuts and Bolts

But before you decide to start a blog in order to quit your day job, make sure your topic is actually useful or interesting to some segment of humanity.

My favorite blogs are about fitness, the paleo diet, lifestyle design, memory techniques, marketing and the economy.

Hardly obscure niches, for the most part.

On the other hand, I'm sure you can make money on something pretty obscure. Especially if people are willing to spend money on it – and if there's not much competition.

And if you absolutely must write a personal blog, or a blog about something that's not immediately useful to many, well...

Best of luck.

I'm not pretending to have a monopoly on great blogging ideas.

I've been wrong so many times it's ridiculous.

If you break all these rules and still manage to become successful, my hat goes off to you. And I'll be happy to buy you dinner so we can talk about it.

(Important caveat: just try to be a "successful" blogger while breaking **rule #1 – just get started**. Go ahead, punk. Make my goddamn day.)

And finally...

Rule #3 – Write like you speak

A blog post isn't a formal letter.

It isn't a 5 paragraph essay.

It isn't a chance to prove how big your vocabulary is or how educated you are.

Nobody cares.

Part 1: Nuts and Bolts

In a way, this point is a continuation of the previous idea of thinking about your audience. Because you need to be real.

I don't care how smart you **think** you are.

If you have a potential audience (and I hope you do)...

They're not sitting at home hoping you'll publish some massive wall of text for them to sift their way through.

They're not hoping they'll have to pick up a dictionary to decipher your meaning.

And they're certainly not going to read whatever you have to write just because you're you and you wrote it.

(Unless you're Kanye West – or someone similarly famous. In which case, congratulations. None of the normal rules apply to you.)

One of the most important things you can do as a blogger is to write like you talk.

Keep it simple, stupid.

And while you're at it, just imagine that your audience is stupid also.

This is not because a lot of people reading your blog will necessarily be dumb – that's a different question, about which I have no comment...

It's simply because we all have other things to do rather than read your blog.

I'm sorry.

But we've all got 24 other browser tabs open, a pot of coffee on the stove, text messages are coming in from people we're hoping (someday) to sleep with, we're reading your blog on our mobiles while on the bus, on the metro, or on the toilet.

You've got like 3 seconds to drag us into your post – or you're gone.

So don't bore us.

Some people see my one-sentence (or one-word) paragraphs, and flip the fuck out. They think I can't possibly be a serious writer.

Well, that's up for debate. (And after all, **they're** the ones commenting on **my** blog.)

But serious or not, I am a **paid** writer. I'm doing this for the creative expression, for the recognition, for the money, for the satisfaction of helping people to achieve their goals... Lots of reasons.

But I'm **not** doing it for a pat on the head from my 8th grade English teacher... or the internet's herd of amateur grammar Nazis.

By the way... the reason for my one-sentence paragraphs is to **break up the wall of text**. Nobody wants to read that shit.

White space, y'all.

And almost nobody speaks in complete paragraphs with an introductory sentence and thesis statement.

So I'm not gonna write that way.

Final thoughts about how to blog good and change the world in the process

Yeah, I just dropped a Zoolander reference up in this. Kinda.

Anyway, before I finish... get a few books about writing and style, and read them. I personally don't like Strunk and White that much, but whatever. Lots of smart writers swear by it.

It has one good line, at least: **Omit needless words.**

Just do that and you'll be ahead of the game.

Aside from Stephen King's *On Writing*, I recommend *On Writing Well* by William Zinsser, and *Writing Down the Bones* by Natalie Goldberg.

Both really good and full of useful ideas.

I probably wouldn't be a writer at all if it wasn't for a copy of

Part 1: Nuts and Bolts

Writing Down the Bones I grabbed from a shelf at a coffeeshop a million years ago. (Thanks Natalie!)

And to finish up, here's my final big tip for today: **read a blog post aloud before publishing it.**

I almost always do, and I almost always find several things that just don't sound natural.

If it doesn't sound natural coming out of your mouth, it won't sound any better in the reading.

Okay?

Ready, set, blog!

You started that WordPress yet?

Everyone and their grandma is a wannablogger these days – just write those ten posts and you'll be ahead of almost all of them.

Moving on...

Part 1: Nuts and Bolts

Massive Action and Tiny Excuses

My friend Anthony Metivier of MagneticMemoryMethod.com recently accused me – on a public forum no less – of taking massive action.

"Massive action like all the gurus recommend."

Originally I thought he was just being nice... because I didn't see it. But the thought kept gnawing at me.

Is anything I've done, any action I've taken, really that massive?

It took me a day of contemplation to come around...

But then I decided he was right.

Here's what most bloggers do: they blog every couple of weeks, or every couple of months.

In other words, when they feel like it.

Here's what I did starting out: I posted a few times a week. Sometimes every day. Sometimes twice a day. I wrote about a dozen books, a thousand articles, and I made 4 or 5 online courses and 200 YouTube videos.

All while holding down my miserable day job.

I'm not sure how I did it.

But at the time it seemed easy.

Or at least easier than waking up in 20 years and realizing that most of my life had gone by in a cubicle, working towards nothing and following the rules in some employee manual.

So...

Massive action works.

Part 1: Nuts and Bolts

But here's the thing: massive action is just small action, built up over time.

One thing I've discovered through writing so many books is that "I'm going to write a book" is a horrible goal to have. It's too big. It paralyzes me just to think about it.

On the other hand, "write 1000 words for the new book" is totally manageable. I can do that in a couple of hours.

And guess what. 1000 words today, 1000 words tomorrow... after a while I've got enough to reasonably call it a book.

By the way... when I talk about all the massive action I took in order to quit my day job, I'm not saying your journey will be the same. A lot of my older articles are total crap, and some of them aren't even 100 words long. Calling them "articles" now seems like a bit of an exaggeration.

So if you're able to do it better and faster than me, great!

Congratulations. I'll buy you lunch. 'Cause you're awesome.

Keep in mind: I started all this with virtually no tech knowledge, and I'm blogging for a market where a lot of people don't even have bank accounts – much less credit cards – and have never bought anything online.

If I can get people here in Spain – as well as in Costa Rica, El Salvador, Argentina and Perú – to spend their hard-earned money on my information products, I don't see what's holding you back.

Remember when we talked about ditching your excuses?

Well, guess what... I'm standing behind that.

'Cause I'm a college dropout who couldn't get a job at McDonald's. I started blogging a couple weeks after getting an internet connection at home for the first time. On a computer with a broken screen that had been left by a friend who skipped town. I bought my own computer later.

I still don't know shit about technology. I can type, and that's basically it.

Part 1: Nuts and Bolts

If we want to talk about my qualifications as an English guru, you should know that I did a 4-week teacher training course back in the early part of the century. I routinely get questions from people who are studying degrees in philology and I have to google key grammar terms just to find out what they're talking about.

Secretly, I think of this as an advantage. Knowing a lot about the complexities of grammar and phonetics doesn't help you speak a language. You just gotta practice: listen, read, speak, write.

Basically: just grow a pair, and get out into the world to communicate.

That's the key to language learning. And you don't need a Master's degree to do it.

As it turns out, it's also the key to blogging. Just grow a pair. (Balls, ovaries, whatever...)

I don't know html. I don't know how to program an online store. And it doesn't matter. There are millions of computer whizzes out there who are making blogs and online stores easy to use... so that people like me can set one up without becoming experts in CSS or Joomla or whatever.

All I have to do is write, take photos, make videos and click publish. The computer whizzes do the rest. (Love you guys – and gals! Without you, none of this would be possible.)

These days, when I go to get a coffee in the morning, I look at the barista and think: if things had gone a little bit differently, I could still be doing that. Making cappuiccinos and emptying trash cans and wearing and apron.

Then I throw 50 cents in the tip jar and go about my day.

Because there are no excuses.

For every excuse or obstacle you can come up with, there's somebody else who's overcome it and gone on to great things.

Part 1: Nuts and Bolts

Everyone you admire...

Think about it.

You admire them because they overcame their obstacles and did something great.

Nobody admires the person with the comfortable life who never had to strive to be better. Those are the coked up kids of your rich neighbors who never make anything of themselves because they don't have to. The trust-fund babies who go to India to find themselves and just end up as useless drugged-out bohemians. Fuck 'em all. Nobody admires those assholes.

So here's what I'm trying to say.

I want you to go out there and take massive action through many small actions.

And do anything you can to get over your excusitis.

Take responsibility.

Because – at the risk of repeating myself – nobody else is going to come along and wave the magic wand that solves all your problems.

Oh, and by the way. I couldn't do this without mentioning Jon Morrow. He's one of the biggest bloggers there is. And he's completely paralyzed, except for his face. He's made millions of dollars from his wheelchair, using voice-recognition software and a mouse he can move with his lips.

He's the blogging world's answer to Stephen Hawking. Just google "7 life lessons from a guy who can't move anything but his face". Or go here: unstoppable.me/life-lessons

Read it and come back.

Done?

Ok, now what excuses do you have left?

Yeah.

That's what I thought.

Part 1: Nuts and Bolts

Sturgeon's Law

Ok. So.

You've made it this far in your blogging journey.

You've thought about a topic.

You've thought about your audience.

You've sat down and made a list of 10 posts you could write.

You've even written one or two of them. But you felt like you needed more... A kick in the pants from a profane, bearded guy with a lot of experience, maybe.

Well, never fear: **Daniel is here!**

I've got a lot more to say about blogging... this could, in fact, be a whole new career for me. Daniel the Blogging Guru.

I can see it now. Me... wearing a suit for the second time in my life. On the front page of some horrific commercial blog. Making big promises.

The lazy man's way to riches. How to earn money on the beach and – occasionally – clean *piña colada* out of a keyboard.

How to wake up alone and freezing cold in any major world city... all through the power of blogging!

Or something like that.

(I'm still working on the tag line.)

Anyway, if you haven't figured it out yet... Tony Robbins I am not.

But of course, I've been around the block. And I believe in you.

So let's go...

Part 1: Nuts and Bolts

Embrace Sturgeon's Law: kill your inner perfectionist

A blog is an imperfect thing.

And over time it will keep evolving.

Many people use perfectionism as an excuse to do nothing.

"No, I couldn't possibly release anything into the world that's less than perfect", they say. "I prefer to do nothing at all!"

To them I say: **you suck.**

Recently, in fact, I heard of something called Sturgeon's Law.

Sturgeon, a science fiction writer, is credited with saying that 90% of everything is crap.

And that's okay.

(Actually, Sturgeon used the word "crud". 'Cause I guess "crap" sounded too offensive. What a pussy.)

(Full disclosure: I considered using the word "wuss" in the last paragraph, but that would defeat the whole purpose. So you got the p-word. Sorry. I'll go sit in the corner.)

Anyway...

The thing about the creative life is that you have to accept sucking at first. You're gonna suck, possibly for a long time, before you get good.

But if you let your inner perfectionist keep you from creating anything at all, well then, **you just suck.**

Period.

Short story: when I was a teenager, I was in a shitty punk band. I was the singer / songwriter / guitarist. When I say we were shitty, I feel like that was largely my fault. Because I sucked at everything except the guitar part. I had no idea how to write songs.

Part 1: Nuts and Bolts

But then again, I think I wrote a total of six bad punk songs in my whole "career" as a musician.

Nobody had told me, back in those days, about the power of 10,000 hours or deliberate practice. Did John Lennon's first six songs change music forever?

Probably not.

What if I had written another hundred songs? I could have escaped the suck and become a rock star and sex symbol. (Or not.)

Anyway...

If blogging is worth doing well, then it's worth doing badly in the beginning.

Kill your inner perfectionist. Or at the very least, immobilize him (her?) with duct tape and a ball gag and lock him / her up in your mental broom closet.

Let the perfectionist out when it's time to scrub the floor or make lasagna.

Because writing will always be imperfect.

A good writer is able to get over the fear, and just let something imperfect out into the world.

Which brings us to our next point...

Embrace the process of constant improvement

If you're publishing a book, and your first print run is 500,000 copies, you'd better make sure you've done your editing.

On a blog, well, it's not quite so important.

You can always go back and rework things later.

These days, in fact, I spend a couple of hours every week going through old posts and making them better.

Part 1: Nuts and Bolts

I guess at the time I wrote them they seemed pretty good. Writing in a foreign language (which is still my moneymaker... writing about English grammar in Spanish) isn't easy, and I was doing my best.

And on my "fun" blog, The Chorizo Chronicles, well... I was used to nobody reading my articles anyway.

Now I have a much larger audience, and when I look at things I wrote 5 years ago, often they're embarrassing.

They suck!

The great thing about a blog, though, is that you can go back and edit old posts and pages. You're not stuck with something you wrote years ago.

You're better than you were 5 years ago. Now make the post better!

Here's the thing: bloggers are expected to be real people, with imperfections. People who read blogs understand they're dealing with somebody who's usually working on their own – not a major corporation with a huge team behind every press release.

People will forgive you for being less than perfect.

And when you're starting out, you can suck all you want.

Feel free!

Because (sorry to say this) nobody's going to be reading your stuff anyway.

A couple of dozen people, tops. Hopefully you at least have friends you can spam about your new posts in the beginning.

And listen: if you can't suck in front of a couple of dozen people you know, you're not going to get anywhere in life anyway.

These days, when I write things, I know that thousands or tens of thousands of people are going to read them. If I include a typo, I'm going to get dozens of emails about it.

Part 1: Nuts and Bolts

I have to think a lot harder before I click "publish", just because I've been in the game longer and I have a bigger audience.

But you – unless you're already famous – don't.

Sometimes, I'd kill to go back to the no-pressure days when I knew I could only possibly piss off a dozen people with a post. Now it could be hundreds... Or thousands!

So you, young blogger... I encourage you to enjoy being on the small stage while you can.

Kill that perfectionist, and embrace the process.

And finally...

Don't imitate – just be yourself

I know, I know.

"Just be yourself" is maybe the world's worst advice.

It's also, often, some pretty **good advice**.

Perhaps we should reword it to "be authentic, and don't be afraid to be the **best version** of yourself".

One of the problems with the advice "just be yourself" is that it's impossible to really be anyone else.

If I wake up with a hangover and an overdue credit card payment on a Tuesday morning and feel like I'm totally sick of being Daniel Welsch, well...

I'm fucked.

'Cause I can't just drop everything and decide to be Ryan Gosling instead.

This goes for your life as a blogger, too.

I wouldn't mind having Tim Ferriss' muscles and millions of dollars. I'd be happy to kick it with Arnold Schwarzenegger and Jamie Foxx.

Part 1: Nuts and Bolts

But at best, if I tried, I could be **a really bad imitation** of ol' Timmy.

Because he's got a monopoly on the Tim Ferriss brand that I'm just not going to beat. (Not to mention, he purposely invented "lifestyle design" in order to avoid competing in an existing market. Which is a level of genius I have yet to replicate.)

Anyway, a blog is a unique opportunity to be authentic. To be you, warts and all.

Nobody's perfect. Nobody else is ever going to be "you".

And nobody else is going to be me, either.

Because...

I'm a superhero, dammit

I love going to other people's blogs for inspiration, and to check out what they're doing. Hanging out with other bloggers is a great way to figure out what's going on in the industry.

But you've still gotta find your unique voice.

You've still gotta do what you're best at.

Your unique experiences and talents are different than everyone else's. Your warts are what makes you interesting.

I like to think of my blogging personas – both Mr Chorizo and English Guru Daniel – as superheroes.

Every superhero has an origin story. Every superhero has powers. And every superhero has a serious weakness or two. Without kryptonite and his shy, under-sexed alter ego, Superman would be a boring story about a guy who's better than everyone.

But he he has his powers AND his weaknesses. He has an origin story on another planet. He stands for something and (just as important) **against** something.

Part 1: Nuts and Bolts

The combination of all that is what makes characters like Superman or Wolverine among the most popular and enduring in literature.

(Sorry, Shakespeare. But nobody's buying their kid a Hamlet action figure or King Lear pyjamas for Christmas.)

Your blogging persona will be a bit different than your real-life persona, because of course you can't express your full personality in 1200 words.

That's why you should curate a bit and decide what you're going to express.

Like I said, it probably shouldn't be some perfect, idealized version of you – if your blog is even about you, to begin with.

My money-making blogs are about English grammar.

It's mind-numbingly boring, at times.

I get questions from people who seem to think it's of the utmost importance to learn the difference between **nonetheless, nevertheless** and **notwithstanding,** and I just want to cry.

But even with my boring topic, I'm able to let my personality shine through: just a normal guy from Arizona who likes steak and wine and girls. Moved to Spain by accident, learned Spanish, now teaches English and helps people stand up against the scammers and charlatans in the language learning space.

I'm not Batman, but I'm the kind of guy a lot of people want to be... or at least my public face is that guy.

And that's what allows me to make a living from teaching English online, despite the fact that I don't have a degree from Oxford or any relevant "qualifications" that give me the "right" to be a grammar guru.

So yeah. Just be you.

And if "you" sucks, remember. You're always changing anyway. Why not change for the better? And while you're changing, blog about it.

Part 1: Nuts and Bolts

Just remember... whatever you do, have some fun with it!

'Cause life is short. Way too short to spend your time being miserable and not pursuing your dreams.

In conclusion, or something...

So. What do we have so far?

You've gotta sit down and write. You've gotta think about your audience and whether they actually need or want what you're writing about.

And after that, you've basically just gotta embrace Sturgeon's law, overcome your fear of rejection, failure and sucking in public.

Kill that perfectionist and put something out there.

When you really think about it, all the creators you admire have probably already put in their 10000 hours before you ever hear of them.

After years of hard work and deliberate practice, suddenly...

Overnight success.

I've asked several people who seem to be overnight successes about this. Because I see what they've done in so little time and I feel dumb. What's their secret?

Actually, as it turns out, their secret is that they put in a lot of hard work. For years. While nobody was watching.

My best pro-blogger friends were writing and blogging anonymously, 10 years ago back in college. They'd paid their dues already. And when they suddenly became successful, it only looked sudden to everyone else.

They did the work. And now they're reaping the rewards.

So there.

Part 1: Nuts and Bolts

Logos, design, and themes for your blog

Here's the most common "mistake" I see among potential new bloggers (or online entrepreneurs in general). And I hesitate to even call it a mistake, because mistake sounds like something small and manageable.

This is slow painful failure. And you're not gonna manage it. It's death.

Here's what they do:

1. Spend the first 3 months thinking about the name of their future blog or business.

2. Spend the next three months worrying about logo design and getting some business cards printed up.

3. Find a friend who's a web designer and willing to make them a custom website for the low low price of only several hundred dollars. But unfortunately the web designer friend is out of town this month and next month has a lot of work, so they decide to finally launch their blog at the end of summer, which quickly gets pushed back to the beginning of next year, etc.

4. Finally, a year later, maybe they get around to writing / making something.

5. They continue blogging or creating, sporadically, when they feel like it. And then they wonder why the money's not rolling in.

Stop.

Just stop now.

If any of that sounds like you, you're doing it wrong.

Part 1: Nuts and Bolts

Because look: I've made it this far with virtually no design. I have business cards which make me look slightly important, but let me tell you: as far as I know, I've never gotten any business from handing them out.

I think it was Gary Vaynerchuk who said something along the lines of "Listen to an old interview with Steve Jobs, or an interview today with Richard Branson... And try to find where they said that the secret to their early success consisted in handing out a lot of business cards. You won't find it. Because nobody's **ever** built their success on handing out business cards."

Listen: I don't even have a logo. I mean, I've had a couple of logos made by friends or people on Fiverr, but I don't like either of them enough to have used them very long.

Also, if you go to one of my websites, you'll notice that for the most part my "theme" consists of black text on a white background.

Only recently did I start paying for a premium theme with all the bells and whistles – but even so, it's mostly that: black text, white background. All the bells and whistles are back-end stuff.

It's not that I'm anti-design or anything. Design is important up to a certain point – and with some things it's very important.

It's just that NOBODY CARES.

It's a little trite to say it at this point, but content is king.

Make good content. Make content people want to share. Make content people want to comment on, and content that makes them want to know more about you. Make content people feel strongly about.

'Cause here's the thing: nobody's bonding with your logo or your impeccable choice of fonts.

Even logos we all know, like the Nike Swoosh, would be nothing without the billions of dollars Nike's spent over the years to associate them to positive qualities. Don't have billions of dollars

Part 1: Nuts and Bolts

like Nike? Well, guess what... you're gonna have to do branding in a different way. And your logo probably isn't that important.

Another fun fact: I've had tons of traffic on my main site for years, and I've done a few complete redesigns with a change of theme. And guess how many people EVER commented about the whole appearance of my website changing from one day to the next?

It's a nice round number: zero.

Yup.

Nobody cares and it's likely that nobody even noticed.

Now I know what you're thinking... All the important bloggers have some super-pro design with a huge video at the top of their website that means the page takes 12 seconds to load but makes them seem so far ahead of the curve it's ridiculous.

My answer: not all. I can think of at least three big-time bloggers who keep it completely simple: James Clear at jamesclear.com, Leo Babauta at zenhabits.net and Mark Manson at markmanson.net.

There are definitely some important bloggers who have big fancy designs – but is the design what hooks people?

I doubt it.

Let me give you my personal reasons for not going that direction with my blogs...

1. As I said before, for the most part nobody cares.

They want the actual content to be useful or interesting, and the theme isn't what's going to keep them coming back for more – or make them whip out their credit card.

2. I couldn't do it myself.

If I wanted an expensive design, I'd need an expensive designer. And once they were done I'd have no idea how to use my own website. I'd have to call them up every time I wanted to change the appearance of my blog. And then deal with them being out of town or having a lot of other things to do. (The big time bloggers often have webmasters on contract, which is just not practical for someone starting out.)

3. The internet is always changing.

What looks cool now might look super dorky in a year or two. And if you just paid a thousand bucks and spent 6 months getting the design perfect, you're not going to want to change it.

4. A lot of traffic's going to mobile...

And most of those fancy themes don't look any different than a free theme once you're looking at them on a screen that's 3 inches wide.

So here's what I recommend: get a free theme, or spring for a "premium" theme in the $50 to $100 range.

Then focus on content.

I've been using Thrive Themes for about a year now and I'm really happy. I pay a yearly subscription of around $100 and I can use their themes on multiple websites.

But before that, I made it 6 years on free themes from the WordPress and tumblr theme galleries.

So there.

Creating content that people want, need, and care about should always be your top priority. Design shouldn't.

If your content sucks you're not going to hook them with your awesome design. If your design sucks you still might hook them with your awesome content.

Now get back to work.

Next up... we're finally gonna talk about money.

Part 1: Nuts and Bolts

How to monetize your blog

As I've mentioned...

I'm a full-time blogger these days. And I have to say: getting here wasn't easy.

Making money online isn't exactly a get-rich-quick type thing. It takes time and effort. Anybody who tells you otherwise is lying.

And probably trying to sell you his online course.

The reality is, it's work. I know several people who make a living through blogging, and some of them do pretty well.

But none of them got there without time and effort.

Caveat #1: Don't let me stop you from trying to get rich quick through blogging. If you **do** make it work, good for you! I'll buy you dinner next time you're in Madrid. And ask you lots of questions about how you made it happen.

Ok, ready for the meat?

Let's go...

There are lots of different ways to monetize your blog, but they can be broken down into a few basic categories.

Here are my top 5 ways to monetize a blog...

I've tried them all, failed at some, and had incredible success with others. And here, I'll tell you about a few of the pros and cons of each.

Ready?

Here's #1...

Part 1: Nuts and Bolts

Monetize your blog through ads

Most people think of advertising as a great way to make money with a blog. And it was the first thing I tried too.

But here's the truth: you need **a lot of traffic** to make money with ads.

You can set up a Google AdSense account in a few minutes, and add some banners or sidebar ads to your website with close to zero technical knowledge...

But you're only going to earn a few cents per click.

Same with YouTube.

I can tell you all about it: I'm probably more YouTube famous than anybody else you know, but the money I make from pre-roll ads ain't gonna put my (future) kids through Harvard.

Sorry, Daniel Junior.

You're just gonna have to find yourself a sugar daddy.

Or go to Arizona State. Your choice.

Anyway, you can always give monetizing through ads a shot. Some niches pay more for clicks than others, and having some income from your blog is better than having no income.

Which brings us to...

Monetizing your blog by selling sponsored posts

If your blog gets enough traffic, it'll start attracting the attention of leeches and other bottom-feeding invertebrates of the marketing world.

They'll send you emails along the lines of:

Dear Webmaster: Your blog would be perfect for my brand. Please take several hours of your valuable time to write a post about my company's new product. In exchange, your blog will benefit from the valuable content that you have created yourself, which I'm sure your readers will find useful and entertaining. Sincerely yours, an uncalibrated weirdo who didn't even bother to find your name.

You can comfortably ignore those people, but even more fun is to use FBI hostage negotiating tactics on them. Check out a book called *Never Split the Difference* by Chris Voss for more about that.

Some companies, of course, are happy to pay for promoted posts. If you can work something out, it's probably going to be profitable for both of you. The reach and popularity of some bloggers makes advertising with them a no-brainer.

(And of course, if you'd like to sponsor a post with me, just get in touch. But be prepared... you're gonna have to pay me.)

Caveat #2: Don't sell links. Google will hate you forever. And if you're a blogger, you'd better stay on Google's good side. If you do a promoted post, mark it as such and make the links "nofollow".

Of course, there's a whole online debate in which business owners say that bloggers suck and just want free stuff, and bloggers say that business owners suck and just want free advertising. And both sides make good points.

(You know who definitely sucks? Yo mama.)

Ahem... sorry. I just realized I'd written several hundred words since my last burst of juvenile humor.

Anyway, I don't do a lot of this – I try to blog about stuff I like and services I actually use. But I might someday do more.

Here's another...

Becoming an expert in your field

I'm definitely biased, but I think basically everyone should have a blog.

Part 1: Nuts and Bolts

And if you're a professional or creative of any kind and don't have a blog, you'd better get one.

Now.

No tech skills? No problem! Send me money and I'll hold your hand through the whole process.

It kills me when I meet doctors, dentists, actors, musicians, businesspeople – anybody really – and they don't have a blog. Just get yourname.com and put up a photo and a copy of your CV.

Please.

Pretty please.

There's no downside – and potentially a lot of upside to building an online presence.

All that being said, my first idea for monetizing my blog was to use it to raise prices for my private lessons. And it didn't work as well as I had hoped – mostly because the economy was collapsing in the meantime.

But having a blog with quality content is a great way to demonstrate your expertise and raise your profile in your field – whatever that may be. And being (or becoming) an expert could lead to coaching or consulting, paid speaking gigs, and more.

Blogging will also send opportunities your way in the form of paying gigs – I ended up writing for Lonely Planet after the editor up in London found my articles about Madrid.

When I was a young dropout, that was my dream job – and they never would have hired me. But years later, I got it, through the power of blogging.

Anyway, just being out there for people to see you is always worthwhile... I've met lots of cool people (and a couple of girlfriends) just by being "that guy with the website".

You can also...

Part 1: Nuts and Bolts

Make money online with affiliate links

A popular way to monetize your blog is through affiliate marketing and linking to other people's products.

Caveat #3: I'm no expert in affiliate marketing and apparently if you want to do it well, it's a full-time job in its own right.

One of the simplest and most obvious ways to make money is to sign up for Amazon Associates and then put a couple of links to different things in every post.

Other popular affiliate programs are for web hosts like Bluehost (good for beginners) and my new host, Siteground, who I love.

And a lot of other companies offer affiliate programs to bloggers or really whoever. I use (and recommend) booking.com when I travel and they offer both a "refer your friends" program as well as an affiliate program.

I think AirBnB has something similar.

And while we're being all James Bondish and international, you can send money with Transferwise and get your first transfer free… if you use a friend's affiliate link.

I love Transferwise. Email me and I'll send you an affiliate link you can use.

What I'm saying is, you can certainly find something in your niche out there to sell or recommend to people.

Caveat #4: The FTC requires bloggers to "disclose a material relationship" if there is one. Meaning, you should tell people that a link is an affiliate link, so they know the score.

A lot of bloggers take this information and go as far as to make a big deal about it every time they post a non-affiliate link too. To me, this screams "Look! I'm such a superior person that I linked to this product or service with no financial motive whatsoever. Please pat me on the back for keeping it so real."

Whatevs, bro.

Part 1: Nuts and Bolts

pat, pat

And finally, the nuclear option...

Make and sell something

I saved the best for last.

Affiliate linking is great for "passive income" if you want to monetize your blog, but creating and selling your own products is where the real money's at.

My first product was a short ebook, which sold enough to make me want to write several more short ebooks.

After that, I branched out into online courses.

And when those were successful, I started a subscription. Having people's cards charged automatically every month is awesome. You wouldn't believe how good it feels.

(That's what she said.)

Caveat #5: Most of my actual selling happens through email, and I use the blog to capture email addresses of potential customers. All that massive traffic on the blog brings me some passive income – through links to Amazon or my online store – but my life of luxury is paid for by email launches where I beat people over the head with my offer until they buy.

Doesn't sound particularly romantic if I put it that way, but hey. It's better than working at the carwash back home.

Anyway, you can sell virtual products, physical products, whatever you want. These days it's pretty easy to set up an online store of some kind and make it happen. If you're doing physical products, Amazon can even do the fulfillment (inventory, shipping, all that) for you.

For digital downloads, I mostly use Gumroad. It's ridiculously easy to set up, and they pay every week...

If somebody buys something, that is.

And anyway, learning how to sell will improve every other aspect of your life. Because so many things are a form of sales or negotiation, and upping your skills can only be a good thing.

Either way, don't worry: there's no magic in any of what I do.

If I can do it, anyone can do it.

Products take time to make, and the first few times you ask perfect strangers to buy your creation can be nerve-wracking. To say the least.

But in the end it's worth it.

And that's where I am now…

Today's just a typical day in the life of a digital nomad and pro blogger…

Spent rolling around on stacks of money, and kickin' it at 5-star hotels, while a whole harem of YouTube groupies and Instagram models fan me with palm fronds and feed me grapes.

I like it when they call me Big Poppa.

Okay, okay.

It's not exactly that.

But I do get to travel a lot, and I've worked from some of the finest second-tier hotels in Europe. (My sexscapades with YouTube groupies will be the topic of the Daniel Welsch biopic coming out in 2027… maybe.)

In any case, what I like best about the pro-blogger lifestyle is that I've been able to fire my boss, meet new people, and set my own schedule… Plus make more money than I ever would have as a "real teacher".

And some final caveats…

There are some final things you should take into account before you start trying to monetize your blog.

Part 1: Nuts and Bolts

For one: what's your strategy for getting traffic?

With no eyeballs on your site, even the best offer isn't going to sell. And for ads or sponsored posts, you need traffic as well. Are you going to be buying traffic on Facebook? Learning SEO? Get an idea of your options and pick one or two. Then execute.

Also: is your niche even monetizable?

I guess on Amazon you can find products for any conceivable interest.

But some niches are easier to monetize than others. Guess what? They're also highly competitive.

Lookin' at you, mommy bloggers.

And finally: does your blog or product meet a need? Does anybody want it? Is there an aspirational or lifestyle aspect?

Without those things, it's gonna be pretty hard to get people to read or buy. People have gotta actually want what you're selling... or affiliate linking to.

And to wrap this up...

I'm convinced that anyone can learn how to monetize a blog.

It's not magic.

But there are certain things you need to take into account. Maybe not every blog is really "monetizable" – and the ones that are will still take some work.

Conversion rates are generally not great, so you have to focus on getting more eyeballs on your site.

And the internet is always changing, so some of the rules might be different soon. (The general principles of marketing aren't changing, 'cause that's just basic psychology.)

But all in all it's quite an adventure, and earning money from a blog offers you a flexibility in your lifestyle that not many other jobs do.

Part 1: Nuts and Bolts

In fact, I wrote most of this chapter on a high-speed train back from holidays in Cádiz. Where I spent 8 days for no reason at all, other than that I could.

Location independence for the win!

Might just start collecting Basquiats, like my dawg Jay Z.

Picasso, baby.

Part 1: Nuts and Bolts

Tools, tips and tricks

This is not going to be particularly technical. If you have specific questions about how to do something, just google it. There are lots of other bloggers out there answering your technical questions. And my technical questions.

Remember: Google is your friend.

In any case, here are some of my favorite tools and services that make blogging easier – or possible…

As long as I've got you here, swing by expatmadrid.com/book and sign up for my emails. I'll send out new tips, new resources and more.

Blogging platforms

There are lots of platforms for blogging, but for several reasons, I recommend WordPress.

For one, you can do almost anything you want with a WordPress.org site. You can choose from hundreds of themes and install any number of plugins that will do nifty things. Most of it's free… you'll just have to pay for hosting and a domain name.

A domain and a year's worth of hosting will probably cost you something in the $50 to $100 range – around $12 for the domain and a few bucks a month for hosting.

In any case, just get started on whatever platform you want. You can always move over to WordPress later on – it's pretty easy.

If you're ready for WordPress now, a site called WPBeginner.com has a lot of content to get you started. Basic tutorials about everything you might need to know.

Part 1: Nuts and Bolts

But if you prefer to start out with something completely free, you can use wordpress.com or tumblr.com to get up and running. Wordpress.com is free and has many of the same functionalities as wordpress.org – but it's hosted on their servers and so they might run a few ads on your site to support the "freemium" plan. And tumblr is just super-simple: text, photos, audio, whatever. Not many options, not much to get confused about. You can even use blogger.com which is owned by Google.

You should still probably buy a domain name, though. If you use one of the above sites to host your blog, the default setting is that your web address will be something like yourblog.wordpress.com – which looks a bit less professional (and is less memorable) than just yourblog.com.

Where to buy a domain name

I used to have my domains at 101domain.com and had no problem with them, except that their website was a bit confusing.

If you live in the US or have a US address you can use, Google Domains is good. It offers free email forwarding so you can have a professional-looking email address forwarded to your Gmail.

You can also use 1and1 and probably a million other services to buy your domain name – it'll cost you about $12 to $20 depending on the extension. And if possible, you should be going for something old school like .com or .net.

Selecting a domain is a whole art and science in and of itself – my recommendation is that it should contain a keyword or two, while still being short and memorable. But plenty of important people are getting by with their own name or with something less than obvious: marksdailyapple.com, for one, is about primal health and written by Mark Sisson.

And there are all kinds of made up words posing as services we all use: Skype, bit.ly, things like that.

Part 1: Nuts and Bolts

Web Hosts

These are the servers that will be hosting your blog once it's up. I personally use (and highly recommend) SiteGround. They have tech support people somewhere in Eastern Europe who will hold your hand through basically anything, and maybe even do it for you.

Some cheaper options are HostGator, 1and1 and Bluehost – if you've seen everybody recommending Bluehost, it's probably because they give out some really aggressive affiliate commissions if you recommend them on your blog.

I personally had a terrible experience with them. But whatever.

Wordpress Plugins

Assuming you're going to use WordPress, there are several plugins you can add that will make your life easier. I'm not going to give a lot of specific recommendations because these things are changing so fast. But I use...

Yoast SEO – SEO (Search Engine Optimization) is how you get ranked in Google. Yoast has a plugin that helps you select keywords and optimize your articles around them. It works.

A lazy-load plugin – this makes it so your pictures only load as needed. If there's one picture at the top of the screen and 12 more that are further down, it only loads the top one. The rest will load as your reader scrolls down. This makes your website faster and easier to use.

A security plugin – there are a lot of them out there, and I don't have any specific recommendations – I think I use a different one for every website I have. But you should definitely use a security plugin. At the very least a plugin that limits login attempts and locks people out. There are a lot of hackers with a lot of bots trying to break into WordPress sites, for whatever reason. Better safe than sorry.

Part 1: Nuts and Bolts

A backup plugin – I personally use one called Updraft, which makes a weekly backup in a zip file that goes automatically to cloud storage on DropBox or Google Drive. I've never needed it yet, but if something ever happens I'm going to be REALLY glad I set that up.

Sumo or some other social plugin – these are just some easy ways to add sharing buttons and an email popup on your site. Make it easier for people to share, and people will share more. Simple. I think if you use a service called Jetpack (which is integrated with WordPress) it has social buttons too. But Sumo's are bigger and therefore – hypothetically – better.

Akismet anti-spam – I use this one specifically. It's free and it blocks 99% of spam comments without you having to ever see them. Works great for filtering out the Viagra and RayBan spam that's still so prevalent online.

Royalty-free photos from Unsplash – I really like a website called unsplash.com for free photos. There are a lot of other places out there too, where you can use photos for free (or cheap). I also search for Creative Commons photos on Flickr and find a lot of good stuff. In any case, if you're hoping other people will respect your copyrights, a good place to start is to respect theirs. So don't just use copyright stuff on your blog without permission.

And that's about it... I use a lot more plugins for more specific things that you probably won't have to do if you're starting out. So don't worry. You can Google it later.

As always, just get started.

Nothing else is gonna happen until you do that.

Part 1: Nuts and Bolts

SEO and Getting Traffic

There are multiple ways of getting traffic for your blog.

And if you're starting out, you should definitely learn about SEO.

If you're not familiar with the term, SEO is Search Engine Optimization – the art and science of optimising your articles and your blog as a whole to show up in Google's search rankings.

If you want the really short version of the story, just go to backlinko.com and do everything Brian Dean says. It'll take some time, but it's worth it.

The slightly longer version is this: get into your ideal readers' heads and think about what they're googling.

Then build your articles around those questions or topics.

Try to get as close as possible to what they'd actually be looking for – using the exact words if you can. There are keywords out there that will help you with this, but I usually just pop something that sounds reasonable into google to see what comes up in "suggested searches".

Back in the day, I had a lot of success just taking the usual questions people asked me in English class and using those as the titles of my articles. If two or three students asked me the same question, I could assume there were tens of thousands of English students around the world who were wondering the same thing. And some of them would be googling it.

After that, you can build your articles around these keywords. Try to focus on long-tail keywords.

For example: good luck ranking for the keyword "London". But you **could** potentially rank for something like "best museums

Part 1: Nuts and Bolts

in London", "top things to do in London", "best sushi restaurants in London", "where to take a Tinder date in London" and things like that.

After that, like I mentioned before, you should install the Yoast SEO plugin.

It will basically give you a checklist of everything you're doing right (and wrong) to make your article rank in Google.

The most important thing, of course, is the title of your article. Your title should contain the keyword – and ideally at the beginning.

After that, use the keyword in the first sentence, and a couple more times in the body of the article.

When you add an image – which you always should – use the keyword as the "alt tag". It's easy to do on WordPress, at the same time you upload the image.

And then do whatever else Yoast says and you'll be golden.

Like I said, you should learn about SEO... but don't just write for the Google bots. Write for your audience, and think about what's going to be useful and interesting to them.

Then go back and make it easier for the Google bots to find you.

Okay?

(Side note: it's embarrassing how many times I have 1200 words written before I even think about a keyword. And then I have to go back and add some random phrase in at 5 different points during the article. If you think keyword first, your life will be easier than mine.)

Now let's talk social...

Part 1: Nuts and Bolts

Social Media

The other big thing you can do to get traffic is to use social media.

Caveat at the beginning: I'm not nearly as good at social as some people I know. So my main advice would be to find some people who are really good at it and try to figure out what they're doing.

In any case, social is always changing... so what I write here could be totally useless by this time next year.

So please... set up a Facebook page. Get into hashtags on Instagram. Pin whatever the hell you want to your Pinterest boards.

But don't spend your whole life on it.

I think the main thing you can use social for is to create discussion and keep yourself on people's radar when you're not selling... so when you do get around to selling something, they already see you as sort of a trusted friend.

More on that in the upcoming chapter "How to become an influencer".

You can also try Facebook ads to get traffic if you're just starting out. But make sure your ad points to a landing page where they can enter their email address. You don't want traffic just for traffic's sake. You want traffic with purpose and intention...

Because you know what they say: "Know what HITS stands for? How Idiots Track Success!"

Ha. Ha. Ha.

Not that funny, actually. But totally true.

Moving on, here's something I'm much better at...

Part 1: Nuts and Bolts

Email marketing

Yeah, I know...

You don't like popups, and I don't like popups.

But when the offer is good and the topic is interesting, I bet you sign up... Don't you? I know I do.

And email marketing is where I actually make money.

Guess how many people spend a few minutes on your blog, think "this is really cool" and then completely forget about you and never come back. What do you think?

I'd put it somewhere in the area of 99%.

But if you can capture those people's emails with a plugin like Sumo or MailMunch and continually update them about both free and paid content, you'll create a relationship with them – and conveniently be able to make offers to them when you're ready to start selling.

Email marketing is a book in itself... I've read more than a few, actually.

For now, I recommend you just set up a MailChimp account at mailchimp.com and start collecting email addresses.

Email them once a week. Be friendly. Use an informal tone.

Whatever you do, don't try to be corporate. Don't bore them. Remember the old sales adage: You can't bore people into buying or sleeping with you.

So just be present, be interesting, and go from there.

MailChimp is great because it's free for your first 2000 subscribers – and by the time you have 2000 people on your list, you should be able to make enough money to pay for it.

Part 1: Nuts and Bolts

One more thing: you want to come up with a better pitch than "subscribe to our newsletter". In email marketing and in everything else, think: what's in it for them?

They don't want your newsletter... they want a solution to whatever problem your blog is supposed to solve for them.

So offer them something in return: "Get my free PDF about the latest apps your hipster friends will all be using soon". "Is the government stealing your Qi? Find out with my new FREE REPORT!"

Wanna see how this works in real life? Stop by my website at expatmadrid.com/book and sign up for my emails. I'll occasionally try to sell you stuff, and you'll see how the pros work. Better yet, it's free!

And that's about all for the nuts and bolts.

Consistency is key... and there's always something else to learn.

Let's move on to the even more fun part: blogger lifestyle.

Onward!

·····PART TWO·····

The Blogger Lifestyle

All the blood, toil, tears and sweat behind the pro blogger lifestyle.

Part 2: The Blogger Lifestyle

A day in the life of a (semi) professional blogger

This is about a year before I quit my job...

7:28 AM

My eyes pop open a full hour before my alarm is supposed to go off. A nameless dread grips me. Oh god, I think. What now? The feeling is in my gut before I even remember why.

Then it hits me:

LAUNCH DAY.

7:37 AM

Hot coffee in my hand, computer warming my junk, I'm back in bed. I open up my sales letter to check if everything's okay.

Fuck me fuck me FUCK ME. This is garbage! This is probably the worst sales letter in history! If I send this out, Gary Halbert is going to appear as a ghost somewhere, to tell a real marketer to come and cut my throat. And they'll totally do it... How are you going to say no to the ghost of Gary Halbert?

[Gary Halbert, for those 99.8% of people who are not aware, is like the Muhammad Ali of direct response marketing.]

8:55 AM

I'm fully caffeinated and my sales letter is looking better.

Still bad (perhaps), but better. At least now it has problem – agitation – solution. It has something about my positioning. I've improved the offer. As Hemingway said, the first draft of anything is shit.

Now it's time for MailChimp.

Part 2: The Blogger Lifestyle

9:28 AM

I've been wrestling with the Chimp for what seems like an eternity.

Checking and re-checking the links. Making sure everything's right.

I still suspect that it's not. And that I'll spend the rest of the day getting unsubscribes. *Spam report! Spam report!* The red lights will be flashing at MailChimp headquarters, like a submarine under attack.

9:31 AM

Finally I'm ready to hit send.

You know what's more horrifying than sending an email out to several thousand people at once? Sending an email out to several thousand people and **asking them to buy something**. Something you spent months creating. Something with your name on the cover. Something with your smiling face on the YouTube video. Your accent speaking a foreign language.

What's worse is the knowledge that it's this, or back to depending on your day job for 100% of your income.

God help me.

Click.

I guess you can't know what it it feels like until you've done it.

9:33 AM

Now, the waiting begins.

I've got a few minutes here to brush my teeth and put on some real pants. And I might as well admit it. I'm clicking refresh on my email every 20 seconds also.

Just in case somebody was just sitting there with their debit card in their hand, waiting up all night to buy this thing.

Part 2: The Blogger Lifestyle

9:51 AM

No response yet. Some people have opened my email, but the click-through rate isn't amazing.

Oh dear Buddha why? Is it my terrible sales copy? Has everybody gone and signed up for a Vaughan Systems course over the weekend?

Am I going to have to go live in one of those flats where you just rent a bed in an 8 hour shift?

What did I do in my past lives to deserve this?

10:00 AM

I'm at the physical therapist. My body's been falling apart at the seams the last few weeks. So I have to pay this guy to put things back in place.

I left my phone at home so I won't think about it. Time to work on this ailing bag of meat and bile called Daniel.

Well, at least my brain is still working. Sort of.

11:00 AM

Time to go home.

The physical therapist says I'll be okay. But I need to sit around with an ice pack, do the stretches and keep coming back for a few more weeks.

And most importantly: no quick movements.

Goody. 32 years old and under orders from a medical professional to hobble around slowly like some old geezer.

11:07 AM

I'm at home. I jump on the computer...

Hot diggity! I made a sale!

Last time I did this, I hit send at 9 AM and then sat around for **four hours**, until a bit after 1 PM, waiting for something to happen. It was torture.

Part 2: The Blogger Lifestyle

So this is already better than that. Of course, it could be a fluke. I still could get my wave of unsubscribes. What's my clickthrough rate again?

11:24 AM

Well, I still might be forgetting to do something. Something big. But I don't have to go to class immediately, and the email doesn't send to Latin America for another few hours.

So, I might as well have some coffee and blog about my angst. 'Cause that's what my generation does. We blog about it.

12:08 PM

Have I mentioned that it's been pouring down rain all morning? Maybe that detail is affecting how I feel a little bit.

I realize that maybe I should write some emails to people I know about this whole thing, to see if they want to tweet about it. "Just tweet about it and hope for the best" is hardly an award-winning marketing strategy, but it's better than sitting here blogging about it.

Meanwhile, a couple more sales have trickled in.

No reason to panic. Yet.

Save draft.

12:51 PM

It's really raining now, and I have to walk down to my first class of the day. I put on a raincoat, stick my well-worn copy of *English Grammar in Use* in a plastic bag, and head out.

It's cold, my feet are soaked, it's windy.

And actually, out here it feels pretty good to be alive.

Maybe I just need to stop hunching over the computer all morning.

Maybe I could get a job as a lifeguard, or a tree surgeon, or a busker. You know, something cool. Not an online marketing guy…

Part 2: The Blogger Lifestyle

1:02 PM

My students start to trickle in. I spend an hour teaching them some of the differences between British and American English.

Like how British people (apparently) get angry about such barbaric Americanisms as "train station," "program" and "gotten".

It's okay.

2:08 PM

I'm back at home.

No sales in the hour and sixteen minutes since I left the house.

I'm a failure! And probably always will be!

I bet Tony Robbins never feels like this.

Then again, Tony Robbins already has his millions. He doesn't have to sit refreshing his email to see if people are sending him small amounts of money.

Tony just sits in his cryotherapy chamber and the money rolls in.

All day long.

Why can't I just be Tony Robbins?

2:20 PM

My lentils are hot on the stove and I sit down to eat.

No sales in the twelve minutes from the time I arrived home till now.

Should I have some more coffee? Should I get drunk?

Stumble into my day job (or, more accurately, my afternoon / evening job) smelling of booze and giggle my way through the first hour and a half of Pre Intermediate 2?

No! There's a lot of day left here. The email just sent to Latin America a few minutes ago. I'm not a total failure yet.

Part 2: The Blogger Lifestyle

2:53 PM

I get my first sale from LatAm. Dolla dolla bill, y'all!

Life is beautiful.

Maybe I should change my socks before I get pneumonia.

Damn, those were some good lentils.

Why am I still sober?

Oh yeah. My afternoon / evening job. Which starts in an hour and a half. Better get used to the idea of going back to work.

3:10 PM

Why phrasal verbs anyway? I spent 22 years of my life without even knowing that phrasal verbs existed! Nobody knows about them, except EFL students.

3:15 PM

I need to get outside.

Better shoes this time.

Movement. Slow, old geezer movement, but movement nonetheless. This day seems like it's taking longer than usual. Time for my afternoon / evening job. *That'll put some spring in my step. Talking to people all afternoon. Sure. It'll be great!*

3:29 PM

More coffee? What exactly am I doing with my life? Why couldn't I stay in Phoenix and get a job at the car wash? I could be manager by now!

I gotta get out of here.

Hey, is that the sun?

Publish.

Part 2: The Blogger Lifestyle

Chop wood, carry water

When I decided I was going to quit my job to go full time, Anthony told me:

"I think you'll find that being your own boss is like the old Buddhist saying. Before enlightenment: chop wood, carry water. After enlightenment: chop wood, carry water."

I had heard the saying... and I thought I understood it.

How wrong I was.

Here's what I think he meant: even achieving your big goals doesn't change much. You still gotta wake up the next day, have some coffee, take a dump, and get to work.

And he was right.

I've reached some pretty unreasonable goals with this whole blogging thing, then turned around and made goals even more unreasonable.

Then I met those.

If I could go back even 5 years and tell under-30 Daniel what his life was going to be like today, he wouldn't believe it for a second.

But here's the thing: I'm basically the same guy.

With a lot of the same problems, same issues and same insecurities as before. Same love handles, same big ears, same unreasonably pale complexion... larger bank balance.

Guess what?

Part 2: The Blogger Lifestyle

The game never ends.

And you've still gotta deal with yourself. Happiness is only partly external – the rest of it's your attitude and the big chemistry experiment that's going on in your brain and gut 24 / 7.

So make sure you eat well, that you still get enough sleep, that you focus on your goals and on the process…

Even after you've fired your boss and achieved your biggest dreams.

'Cause unless you're dead, you've got a lot more you can do in the world.

And it's your obligation to do what you can to make the world a better place… at least occasionally, between piña coladas on the beach.

Ok, sorry. I hate the word obligation. But when I tell people that I help others because it makes **ME** feel good, they invariably say "that's selfish".

So…

Listen up, puritans. It's your **moral fucking obligation** to help others and to make the world a better place.

Do it and feel bad. Or even better, do it and feel good.

Either way: do it.

Now let's talk about the habits that'll get you where you want to go as a writer.

Ready?

Part 2: The Blogger Lifestyle

Good writing habits

Good writing habits can be summed up in a sentence:

Pick a number of words you're going to do every day, and then sit down and write that number of words.

Easy enough, right?

Well, sometimes...

I should elaborate, because there are a couple of nuances to the whole thing. But a lot of "being a writer" really is that simple.

Write more. If possible, write every day. You'll improve.

Stephen King claims, in *On Writing*, that his daily number is 2000 words. That's usually my number too. Since I'm usually working on multiple projects, it often ends up writing 1000 words on one thing in the morning and 1000 words on another in the afternoon.

But if you feel better about it, start small. Do 1000 words a day, or 500. The point is to develop the habit. You can start ramping up your numbers later on.

There are also writers who go by time, or by page count. Some famous Victorian guy (I can never remember who) would go by the clock every day, and stop in the middle of his sentence if time ran out. If he finished the novel he was working on in the middle of his morning writing time, he'd get out a clean piece of paper and start on the next one.

Balls to the wall, famous Victorian guy. That's the way you do it.

Also, we must remember the immortal words of Hemingway: "the first draft of anything is shit."

Part 2: The Blogger Lifestyle

Don't judge your first draft: just get it done.

The important thing is to get all your ideas out of your head and onto paper. Don't censor yourself. You can (and should) edit later.

Good writing happens in the rewriting. So just get the first draft done and then worry about it.

I guess some people out there are wondering about desks and having proper feng shui in your home office or whatever. I personally could care less. My advice: figure out what works for you and do it.

I write a lot of this stuff sitting on my bed or my sofa. I write in cafés and hotel lobbies and on high-speed trains.

Anywhere reasonably quiet, and I'm good to go. And remember: I live in Spain, where reasonably quiet means there's probably a group of people shouting 10 feet away and a garbage truck rumbling by outside the window.

And actually, I don't even own a desk. Buying furniture seems like one of those adult things I can't be bothered about… so I don't. (I do lots of other adult things, like save for retirement and eat broccoli. But still. Furniture, for some reason, seems beyond me.)

Key point: don't let your lack of a "suitable" workspace be an excuse to your progress. Just get started.

Have I said "just get started" enough yet?

Nah. It's probably never going to be enough.

Okay, so you've got your number of words.

Do that today, do that tomorrow. Do that every day you can.

But if you have to skip a day, don't beat yourself up over it. Just sit down the next day and get back to work.

Also, remember Neil Strauss' number one rule:

Part 2: The Blogger Lifestyle

"The #1 rule of writing is this: Nobody cares. Nobody cares about you. They don't care about your thoughts. They don't care about your ideas. They don't care about what you have to say, what you did yesterday... They do not give a shit! And from there... how can you make them care?"

Neil Strauss is one of the biggest ghostwriters and rock journalists out there. Google his talk "The Secrets of Addictive Writing" for a lot more, or watch his interview with Tim Ferriss on Creative Live. Both are worth your time.

So now you're writing every day. You're cranking out blog posts, you're working on that novel, whatever.

Remember what Hemingway said?

Yeah. Your first draft is shit.

That's where the editing comes in. Think about your reader. Omit needless words. Read it aloud. Break up the paragraphs to leave some white space.

Then hit publish.

Good writing is in the re-writing.

And finally: what I said before. And what I will continue saying.

Inspiration is for amateurs. Don't wait.

A lot of my best blog posts started out with a one-sentence idea. 1800 words later, they'd ended up somewhere completely unexpected, and were not even about what I originally thought they would be.

For a while, I was worried that this meant I "wasn't a real writer". So I asked around. Turns out a lot of "real writers" do the same thing...

They just get to work, and the inspiration happens while they're writing. If they knew where it was going before they sat down, they wouldn't have to actually write the thing.

So embrace the process...

And do those daily words.

Part 2: The Blogger Lifestyle

5 things I've been asking myself since becoming a professional blogger

Writing, as Molière said, is like prostitution.

First you do it for love, then for a few close friends, and then for money.

Molière, of course, wasn't on Tumblr. But blogging, to me, feels basically the same.

I've been blogging for about 7 years.

And ever since I went pro, I have this awkward moment of doubt when introducing myself.

Interlocutor: Nice to meet you, Daniel. What do you do?

Me: Well, I'm a professional blogger.

Interlocutor: ...

Me: Oh, you know. Gotta do something.

In my head I'm thinking, *Is blogging even a real job? Should I come up with some sort of euphemism? Why does no-one seem overly impressed when I say it? Is it secretly the dorkiest thing in the universe? Maybe I should have kept my job at the Safeway back home... oh yeah, they fired me. But the carwash seemed interested in an interview.*

Etc etc etc.

In any case, here I am. And these are the questions I've been asking myself, as I lie awake at night, contemplating my strange new pro-blogging existence.

Part 2: The Blogger Lifestyle

1. How exactly did this happen?

It's weird.

I wake up in the mornings, and I write. I sell the stuff I write. And somehow, this has been paying my rent.

I consider myself, all in all, to be incredibly lucky.

I've met dozens, perhaps hundreds, of wannabe writers in my life, as well as a few "real" pro writers, and at this point I can say one thing: what differentiates the pros from the wannabes is pretty simple. We sit our asses down and do the work.

And then, we're willing to put it out and accept the criticism that comes our way.

Ponder this:

Waiting for inspiration is for amateurs.

Credit for that idea should go to Steven Pressfield. It's not exactly a direct quote. But I recommend you read his books *The War of Art,* and / or *Do the work.*

Just trust me.

Or how about this piece of timeless wisdom:

Thinking about being a writer is never going to pay your bills.

Credit for that one: Daniel Welsch. Change "writer" for whatever other creative pursuit you're interested in, and it still applies.

Thinking about being a musician? A painter? A YouTube star?

Well, you'd better actually start practicing and doing the work... 'cause thinking about it isn't going to get you anywhere.

Part 2: The Blogger Lifestyle

2. Is it all just clickbait, in the end?

I don't know.

My working title for this chapter is "Some thoughts on the writing process".

But (and this is a **big but**)...

I know that if I actually publish it with that title, maybe 3 or 4 of my friends will take the time to read it. And otherwise, it'll be condemned to obscurity. And that's okay. I'm content to have parts of my writing mired in the backwaters of the internet, where nobody ever goes except by accident.

But there's another part of me that thinks, "What if there's a **million** aspiring young writers out there who are just dying to bask in the fuzzy glow of my hard-earned wisdom? Aren't I doing them a disservice as long as I stay in the shadows? Shouldn't I do **everything possible** to make sure the warm fuzziness makes it onto their Facebook feed, somehow?"

So I go back and I think of a better headline. Then I re-write the article to fit that headline. Then I re-write the article to make it easier to read.

Then I re-write the article again, to...

Well, you get the idea.

I guess if you're the *New York Times*, you feel some obligation to bore people with headlines in the passive voice and big words that prove you went to college. Maybe it's written down in your style manual.

Kill me now.

I guess it works for them. But I didn't go to college. (Well, barely.) I don't have to please an editor. And the passive voice bores me to tears.

Part 2: The Blogger Lifestyle

I have some respect for the *Times*. Usually. (I wrote an article their style, at one point, just as an exercise. It's called *As Boomers Near Death, Inane Blathering about Millennials Increases.* You can read it if you want: expatmadrid.com/boomers.)

And I don't particularly like clickbait either. But here's the thing. We are here, on the internet, **with 24 other browser windows open**, and if you bore people with the headline they're not going to click. If you bore them with the first sentence, you're done.

Better make it interesting.

I spend a lot of time these days imaging headlines for every situation. I write and rewrite. I read everything aloud before clicking publish. I try to make it simple, imagining that somebody is reading it on the bus, or on the toilet, or whatever.

Without these things, I'd probably be dead broke.

So listen close, aspiring bloggers. **Hard-earned wisdom here:** you've got about 3 seconds to earn someone's interest.

Make the most of it.

3. Am I a sellout?

Maybe.

But thankfully, the part of me that really takes terms like "sellout" seriously died long ago. Writing? Prostitution? As long as it gets me out of having to find a "real" job.

I write for a couple of reasons. One is to help people in more than a hundred countries to learn some English. The other is to pay my rent.

The time when I had a strong opinion about "selling out" is long gone.

And I think it's better that way. Still, when I meet more idealistic people, who write poetry and stories and hope someday to publish a great existential novel, I sort of envy them.

Sort of.

At the very least I remember what that felt like, and I feel like maybe I've lost a little part of myself.

Anyway, as I've mentioned before, I once wrote a novel about my teen angst. I might publish it someday. Under a pseudonym and without telling anybody.

Not only did the process kind of suck, I more than suspect that the result sucks too.

And that was enough novel-writing, at least for the next few decades.

Arguably, the world doesn't much need my articles about English grammar. But if there's something the world needs even less than another grammar article, it's **my novel about teen angst.**

So screw it.

Back to grammar. On the other end of the spectrum...

4. Is this really work? Because it doesn't feel like it...

The lifestyle really is so awesome, most of the time, that I feel a bit guilty.

Thanks, puritan upbringing.

Last year I visited 6 different countries. I wrote one of my most important articles in a historic café in Lisbon. I worked on the design of a new book while in Budapest. I launched an online course while taking a workshop in Amsterdam with my favorite fitness gurus.

Travel is awesome, but earning money while **travelling is pinch-me-I-must-be-dreaming.**

As if that weren't enough, even on my hardest-working days back home, I still have time to spend an hour or two in the park. I can still drink wine with lunch, see my friends when I want (when they're not working!) go to a museum, take a day off, whatever.

If I want to sit around all Tuesday afternoon watching South Park and eating chocolate... guess what?

There's nobody to stop me!

Awesome, awesome, awesome...

It's the *4-Hour Work Week*... But without Tim Ferriss' muscles, millions of dollars or Silicon Valley connections. (Love ya, Tim. I've read your book twice, and it changed my life twice. Thanks!)

In any case, I sometimes feel bad about it.

When I think of my friends sitting at a desk somewhere, never seeing the sun, asking for someone's permission to take a day off. When I wake up for the 30th consecutive day without an alarm. When I can count sitting in the café with a notebook and my Kindle as "work".

It's just really really cool.

Of course, I had to bust my ass to get here. Before going pro with my writing, I was teaching on a schedule that probably would have killed some of the lesser mortals out there. And writing in the hours between classes.

So hey. Maybe it's karma. Maybe doing those 12 hour days for years on end, I've earned it.

Maybe.

Either way, I appreciate the days, the freedom and life in general like never before. Except for the occasional moment of nagging puritan guilt.

And finally...

5. Where do we go from here?

This is the big one. My books were at #1 on Kindle 3 times last year (in Spain and Mexico, to be fair, I think it's a bit easier). And

Part 2: The Blogger Lifestyle

I've knocked a few other big things off my bucket list since going pro.

And now...

I'm living this ridiculously awesome lifestyle, and feeling like I've accomplished most of what I really needed to do in this life.

I had a day back in 2015, before going pro, when I was #1 on Kindle, falling in love, happy with life, and planning an amazing future. And I thought:

It's going to be hard to top this. I should probably just die happy, and soon! Quit while I'm ahead.

Well, I didn't die. (And the girl I was falling in love with dumped me.)

And in fact, people in my family live a really long time.

So I'll probably be around for another few decades. I guess I'd better find something else to do... preferably, something even bigger, better and more meaningful.

What, exactly, will it be?

That's the mystery...

But let's move on.

Part 2: The Blogger Lifestyle

How to become an influencer on Instagram

Influencers.

We've all seen them on Instagram...

Girls whose only apparent talent is looking good in a bikini.

Standing in front of a perfect Mediterranean beach, ass sticking out towards the camera – perhaps to emphasize the vapid inspirational quote.

"If you want to, you can!"

#barf

We click on their profile... Who is this mysterious person?

Sonia. 24. Art student and influencer.

Hmpf.

And if the female posterior isn't your thing, there are also guys playing the influencer game.

Guys with aristocratic noses, who gaze out windows, thoughtfully stroking curated stubble – all in order to show off the $3000 watch that peeks out of the sleeve of their tailored suit.

We click...

Blake. Fashionista. Fitspo and Influencer.

#yourmothermustbesoproud

Who are these people, and how do they manage to get such massive followings? How does one become an influencer?

And all with no apparent skills or abilities?

Part 2: The Blogger Lifestyle

These are the questions that keep me up at night...

Is Paris Hilton controlling your mind?

Of course, this is nothing new.

A decade ago, I was shocked to learn that Paris Hilton earned 5 figures a night just for showing up at certain clubs...

Because business would explode if Paris had been seen partying there.

I don't personally go to clubs, or care much what Paris Hilton does...

But it's interesting.

In my short millennial life, as far as I can tell, Paris Hilton was the first example of somebody who's famous just because she's famous.

Be rich, do nothing, go to parties, and millions of soulless consumer drones will envy you.

They'll want to hang out in the general area of your table at a nightclub. They'll drop $80 on your brand of perfume...

Because your snotty rich aura around a product is all they need to buy it.

Fair enough.

#richkidsofinstagram

The difference between then and now is that way back in the past decade, if you wanted to become an influencer you had to attract the attention of a TV network – you had to sit in meetings and sign contracts and make promises and deal with producers and god knows what else...

All before you got to parade your perfect posterior or chiseled features in front of millions.

Now "anyone" can do it on Instagram – with the help of the right hashtags and a few bots to send out automatic comments.

#atleastthebotsloveme

Anyway...

Warning: you might be under the influence

Perhaps I'm not the right person to be talking about celebrity culture.

When my friends mention anything that's been happening in Miley Cyrus' life, I'm usually puzzled as to how they've found out, or why they'd choose to waste mental space on such data.

(I'll watch her swing around on a giant phallic symbol in the video for Wrecking Ball any time... But that's just me.)

I'm that weird guy who finds out about pop culture 5 to 10 years after the fact, usually through Wikipedia.

However, there are definitely people who influence me.

People who mention a book on their podcast and 4 seconds later I'm buying it on Amazon...

And I guess if there were a nightclub in Madrid where Warren Buffett and Charlie Munger were known to kick it, gangsta style, I'd stand in line.

On the other hand, I'm certainly not running out to buy a Coogi sweater just because Biggie mentions them as a status symbol. And I'm not looking for Jay-Z's favorite brand of sneakers when I'm out shopping – possibly because they'd cost 7 times my budget.

I did once spend an afternoon drinking Remy Martin at the Amsterdam Hilton, in a combined fit of Biggie / Jay Z / John Lennon geekiness.

It was raining like a motherfucker, and drinking Remy at the Hilton seemed like a classy way to stay dry.

Part 2: The Blogger Lifestyle

And as the saying goes, "When the Remy's in the system, ain't no tellin…"

But that's another story.

So…

How to become an influencer in 6 easy steps

I'm the proud owner of Influence and two other books by Robert Cialdini – the 800 pound gorilla of the psychology of persuasion.

And according to Cialdini, one of the 6 main forms of influence is social proof.

In other words, if a lot of other people are doing something, it must be a good idea.

Therefore, if you have 25k (or 2.5m) subscribers on Instagram, you must be "somebody". Or at least **more** somebody than us lesser mortals who count our followers in the hundreds.

These are what the serious social scientists call heuristics.

Rather than deciding if something is a good idea or not on its own merits, we follow the crowd, we do what someone in authority tells us to do, or we just try to stay consistent with what we've said and done in the past.

This saves our brain's valuable processing power for more important things, like watching Miley Cyrus videos and thinking of excuses not to work out.

In other words, people are basically dumb, and we respond to certain stimuli in an automatic, subconscious way, by pulling out our wallets.

Another example…

That hot girl's leaning on the hood of a new Acura?

Then I must immediately purchase an Acura! It's clearly a vehicle of the highest quality. Impeccable Japanese design and workmanship.

Part 2: The Blogger Lifestyle

Duh.

That one's called the halo effect, which Cialdini categorizes under "liking".

If attractive people do something, it's a doubly good idea. They're obviously genetically superior to us commoners, therefore their decisions are probably better.

And seeing Paris Hilton at the club?

That's authority, another one of Cialdini's big six – in the mind of club kids, Paris is an authority on partying.

I guess.

#soerudite

And you won't believe what happened next...

Has Daniel become an influencer?

After writing the preceding paragraphs, I let this article sit for about a month...

Like so much else I do, I didn't know what the hell was the point. And the first draft was so bad it was bringing tears to my eyes.

In the weeks that followed, I started posting lots of photos of places I went on my Instagram and on Facebook.

(You can follow me at instagram.com/danielwelsch if you're so inclined. And by all means, head to facebook.com/chorizochronicles for more blogging stuff.)

Then, I got on focalmark.com for a list of annoying hashtags to use...

#highsnobiety

And I was shocked at the results – I was getting new likes, new followers.

Part 2: The Blogger Lifestyle

It took me a few weeks to realize that it was all bots. If someone comments "awesome post" on my **#dailydogpic** in the quarter second after I've published it, guess what...

They're a bot, not a human.

I was about to give up at the meaninglessness of all this bot-pleasing when I was shocked again...

Because that's when people I know started asking me serious questions about the places I had been and recommended.

About restaurants here in Madrid like Keyaan's Empanadas, or L'Artisan, for example. Should I take my wife there for our tenth anniversary? Is it so expensive that only pro bloggers can afford it?

Things like that.

And then they'd say... "Well, you're an influencer. I saw it on your Instagram, so I figured I'd go."

Um...

Thanks, bro!

I guess I am an influencer, in my own small time way.

And really, we all are – or we all could be.

The only way online influencers get into our heads is by showing up over and over again – in that sense, they're like friends.

Post three times a day, and people will see you. They'll think they know you. They'll value your opinion.

And when you say Remy...

They'll order it the next time they're in da club.

Or at the Amsterdam Hilton.

Part 2: The Blogger Lifestyle

Warning: You probably don't want to be a digital nomad

Ahh, the life of a digital nomad.

You wake up late, and are happy to find yourself in Thailand, just a short walk from the beach. You pour yourself a cup of coffee, answer a couple of emails, and then pull on your flip-flops to wander off and spend the day surfing while your **passive income** rolls in.

By the time you stumble home drunk at 2 AM, your bank balance has grown considerably, you've met all kinds of awesome people, and you're sure that those suckers back home are envying the shit out of you. (In fact, they've been texting you all day to say so.)

Ummm...

Does anybody actually live like that?

Maybe.

I've never been to Thailand.

But from where I'm sitting it seems like a lie.

Here's the truth: **you probably don't want to be a digital nomad.** You probably don't even want to live abroad for any length of time.

I recently read a **brilliant** article by Erick Prince over on Minority Nomad. Here's a pretty link: expatmadrid.com/erick

There's a lot of truth in that article. But first...

Part 2: The Blogger Lifestyle

Just to clear this up at the beginning

I'm not really a digital nomad.

I'm an expat. I've been living here in Madrid, Spain for about 12 years.

For the last year couple of years, I've been making a living exclusively through writing and blogging, which means I'm location independent.

I've travelled a lot since quitting my day job, but I'm not really interested in going full-on digital nomad.

There are several reasons why, and most of them are addressed in Prince's article. So without further ado, my response. Here's why you probably don't want to be a digital nomad (or an expat either).

Some points from Prince's article:

You'll probably be an international criminal

Yup.

Like I said, I've been living abroad since '04. And my current lifestyle would be difficult (if not impossible) if I were trying to follow all the local tax and immigration laws **and** the ones back home to the letter.

Having income and bank accounts in multiple countries sounds cool and James-Bondish, but really it opens up a whole bureaucratic can of worms that you probably don't want to get involved with.

Just trust me.

Wherever you're living, you'll probably at best be in some sort of legal limbo with somebody.

Can you handle it?

Part 2: The Blogger Lifestyle

You have to be a hustler to be a digital nomad

Oh yeah.

I don't know about your digital nomad friends. But the real, legit digital nomads I know work their asses off.

Like the author of the other article says, he has to travel around and hustle to take more pictures even if he doesn't really feel like it. Sometimes the income is sporadic. You can lie around in bed if you feel sick, but if you're anything like me, you have thousands of things to do... and lying around in bed ain't paying the bills.

Personally, I've hung out with Gloria Atanmo from theblogabroad.com (she's about as nomadic as they come) and she works her ass off making travel look like non-stop fun and adventure.

I see how much time she spends on social media and responding to comments and emails, and all I can say is: I don't want her job.

You probably wouldn't either, if you saw what went into it.

Personally, I enjoy the hustle.

Usually.

But sometimes I just wish it would stop.

What about my other friends with online businesses? They also work their asses off. They can be more or less nomadic, but even when they're "on vacation" they're still hard at work for several hours a day.

What about that passive income?

Another point in the article is about passive income.

Well, passive income does exist. It's what you get when you invest in stocks or an index fund, and get paid dividends without lifting a finger.

Part 2: The Blogger Lifestyle

Do the math. Even if you're earning 6% on your money, you need to invest a LOT to be able to spend the next 5 years surfing without going broke.

Another passive income strategy could be to buy an apartment building, hire a manager and head off to the beach to live on other people's rent money.

Don't have hundreds of thousands of bucks sitting around to make either of those plans work?

Well, I'm sorry, but you're probably going to have to work for a living. And work is work, even if you're doing it on a beach in the Canary Islands.

I really like Paula Pant's blog Afford Anything when it comes to financial freedom and passive income. She's into real estate, and I'm not, but she still has a lot of interesting stuff to say.

But guess what?

I'll bet real money that at least some weeks, she works harder on her "passive income strategy" than you do at your day job.

About these people who claim to work an hour a day and then just watch the cash roll in… Maybe they do exist. But they must be people with a few good products, a traffic strategy, and a lot of automation or outsourcing.

And trust me, whatever their workload looks like now, they didn't get there by working one-hour days.

Travel just might bring out your character flaws…

One of the article's best points is about those internet memes where travel is all romantic self-discovery.

Is it?

Uh… kinda. Sometimes.

On the other hand, if you were a miserable asshole back in Vegas, you'll be a miserable asshole in China too. At least after the initial euphoria wears off.

Part 2: The Blogger Lifestyle

Here's one of my favorite quotes from Prince's article:

"Here's what travel will do. It will expose your character flaws. That's for sure. But long term travel, and the privilege that comes with being a "wealthy westerner", gives us the means to reinforce our flaws. Alcoholic? You can get trashed every night and no one will blink. Hell, most places in the world will encourage this. "

Yeah, pretty much.

(Ask me how I know.)

Fact is, all that social pressure to be "normal" back home just sort of disappears abroad.

For me, it's great. I don't have to deal with the opinions of wackjob conservatives or small-minded religious nuts back on the ranch, and I'm much happier.

But some people, apparently, need that social pressure to keep them from turning into (this is the technical term) huge douchebags.

Couple that with the loneliness and rapid turnover in expat social circles, and you might have to prepare yourself for some weirdness from yourself and others.

Reverse culture shock is a bitch

Another quote from the article: "One of the biggest issues you might deal with is coming to the realization that your friends / family are assholes. Or backward minded at best."

Yup.

I haven't spent a lot of time back in the US, but I have had to deal with this online.

People back home just don't understand that **other countries are not the US.** And that we have a million other things to worry about that have nothing to do with what seems so urgent on the other side of the Atlantic.

Part 2: The Blogger Lifestyle

This could make us expats seem like assholes, or maybe make the people back home question our sanity.

And I think there's really no way to bridge this gap and understand each other.

How do you describe a decade living abroad to someone who's barely even left town? Or who feels like a "citizen of the universe" because they've shopped at WalMart in 5 different US states?

Short answer: you don't. They don't have enough experience to understand it.

So: the million-dollar question...

Do you really want to live abroad?

Here's the thing.

I've met a ton of other expats in these years I've lived abroad. And most of them aren't cut out for it. They whine endlessly about how everything in Spain sucks, they get tired of the bad Spanish salary, or the people, or the red tape.

And they go home.

They've had an adventure. Spent a year abroad. And good for them.

Hanging in for the long term, though, is a totally different matter.

Life back home goes on, people forget about you, and here you are, a foreigner in somebody else's home town, wondering what exactly you're doing with your life.

Living abroad is great, but it's not for everybody.

I'd say, as a rough estimate, that the success rate is about 10%.

The rest of those kids are back at home now, telling their friends from high school about that one time they were in Europe,

Part 2: The Blogger Lifestyle

and how cool it was, mincing along the Seine, drinking *sangria* in Seville, whatever.

Listen: you probably don't want to live abroad.

But as usual, that's just what I think.

Almost done here...

Part 2: The Blogger Lifestyle

A day in the life: London Edition

Another day in the life, about 18 months after firing my boss...

5:14 AM

Suddenly I'm awake on the sofa-bed at Jane's house.

Zone 3, West London.

Waking up at random hours of the night doesn't happen to me much anymore... but it does tend to happen when I actually have to get up early.

And today is one of those days.

It's my last day here. And Jane's promised to wake me before leaving for work. In any case, I'm awake 2 hours before her.

After some useless rolling around trying to get back to sleep, I decide to flip on the light. I make some Nescafé and finish editing the video from yesterday.

Then I start writing an accompanying blog post. Today, I'm teaching British slang.

Stonking. The dog's bollocks. Innit?

7:15 AM

I've got enough instant coffee in me that I'm starting to feel optimistic about the day. Also, I find that I'm reading 4 different articles on 4 different tabs, and just skipping back and forth.

Gotta stop that. In a world of multitaskers, single tasking is the new superpower.

And it's a superpower I'm struggling to develop.

Jane's up and in the shower.

Part 2: The Blogger Lifestyle

On the computer, Ramit Sethi says I should raise my prices. Mark Sisson says it's inevitable that one's capacities diminish with age, but suggests living with an edge anyway.

Time to pack my suitcase.

9:30 AM

I'm out the door, headed for the Tube.

On the way out, I meet some sort of typical English woman. Half witch, half deer in the headlights.

She says something incomprehensible – not the first time I find myself unable to understand my own language in London.

On the second try, I understand that she's saying something along the lines of "You want me to get the door?"

I say yes, and head off.

So long, Jane's house!

Soon I'm on the Tube, changing at Victoria Station.

Off at Green Park and out into the hustle of London on Piccadilly. Such an active city. So diverse and so modern and so awesome.

I love Madrid, but London makes Madrid look like some backwater in the middle of nowhere.

It's hard for me to say it, but it's true.

10:30 AM

I've left my suitcase at Jane's office. Time for some real coffee.

I find a place north of Piccadilly Circus where the baristas all call me "buddy".

Double espresso.

Thanks, buddy.

Now that I've got some real caffeine in me, I'm feeling a bit anxious to get back to Madrid and back to work.

Part 2: The Blogger Lifestyle

But why waste my last morning in London sitting in front of the computer?

I might never be back here. At least that's what I usually try to think when I visit places.

And who knows?

If I die tomorrow, I won't regret having so many unanswered emails.

I throw my hard-working side a bone and spend half an hour planning and setting objectives for the new month of March. It's going to be an interesting year.

11:20 AM

I wander towards the north till I hit Oxford Street. London is huge and this shopping street seems at least 5 times longer than anything we have in Madrid. Not to mention the side streets where there are more expensive brands, pubs, cafés, restaurants from every country in the world.

Selfridge's department store is apparently modelled after the Parthenon. Harrods has an Egyptian Room and an Egyptian staircase, not to mention probably a dozen restaurants and a number of bars and cafés. Truffle bar. Prosecco bar. Oyster bar.

It's too bad I'm only vaguely interested in shopping – and that only a few days a year.

I enjoy the ambiance in any case.

Eventually I'm walking past the US Embassy, the statues of Reagan and Roosevelt, and through the fantastically nice neighborhood surrounding.

I briefly think: if I could afford to live in one of these houses, would I?

Probably not. Hopefully I'd come up with something more interesting to do with 4000 pounds a month – or whatever godawful price.

Part 2: The Blogger Lifestyle

But you never know.

1:30 PM

One last sandwich with Jane before the airport.

Quick London lunch.

2 minutes walk, 2 minutes in line, 15 minutes sitting down in the café. I guess this is great for productivity, but I do enjoy a 2-hour Spanish lunch with wine.

2:03 PM

Waiting for the Tube again – this time for Heathrow. London Underground has some pretty funny names for stops.

Goodge Street. Cockfosters. Colliers Wood. Tooting Common. Mudchute.

My sense of humor hasn't matured since I was 12, but whatever.

Mudchute.

Ha!

3:10 PM

Heathrow.

Checkin. Security.

Off with the coat, off with the boots.

Coffee on the other side. I'm in a daze from waking up so early, and decide to work on formatting a new ebook I'm putting together.

Mindless, repetitive, probably outsourceable.

In the middle of formatting, I get a message that my first article is up on Esquire.

Wow!

I click. The paleo diet. "Eat bacon like a modern caveman."

Part 2: The Blogger Lifestyle

Check it out here: expatmadrid.com/paleo

The photo I took looks great...

And I get chills down my spine seeing my name on Esquire.

Ho. Ly. Fuck.

I get a bit teary-eyed contemplating it, then a bit giggly.

I can't believe my good luck sometimes.

Why me?

Honestly, when I started blogging years ago, I never expected to make it this far. I never expected to make it anywhere, really. I just wanted to have a website, thinking it would allow me to charge more for private lessons.

Never expected to end up as a contributor for *Lonely Planet*. Never imagined I'd see my name on *Esquire*.

Tim Ferriss says we tend to overestimate what we can do in a year, but underestimate what we can do in 5 years. And in my experience it's true.

My life now is WAY beyond any "realistic" plan I would have been able to make 5 years ago. I would probably have been somewhat terrified at the thought of so much "success".

But hey.

In 5 years a lot can change.

4:30 PM

I've been sitting around in my state of sleepy euphoria and now I realize I'd better find my gate.

Oops. Turns out it's further than I thought.

I've got 15 minutes to get there. And there are several escalators plus one of those little intra-terminal trains between me and my flight.

My poor little anglosaxon heart is racing. I'm never late for anything.

Part 2: The Blogger Lifestyle

That'll teach me to feel euphoria in an airport.

I make it just in time, as the last people are boarding.

Whew!

5:10 PM

On the plane, and it's delayed. Something about loading luggage into the holds.

The pilot is Spanish, and speaks a kind of informal un-pilotlike English over the PA that's quite endearing.

"We should be taking off in, like, 5 minutes, so thanks for your patience, really, guys."

How do people become pilots? I understand it's quite expensive and involves much study and training.

Those are people with a life plan. People who don't mind spending 10 years on something that might never pay off.

Not like your humble narrator.

5:30 PM

A bit late, but we're in the air.

Adios, London!

I read another chapter of *Cien años de soledad.* Such a great book, and I'm happy to be able to read it in Spanish now.

Como en aquel tiempo no había cementerio en Macondo, pues hasta entonces no había muerto nadie, conservaron el talego con los huesos en espera de que hubiera un lugar digno para sepultarlos, y durante mucho tiempo estorbaron por todas partes y se les encontraba donde menos se suponía, siempre con su cloqueante cacareo de gallina clueca.

That's genius.

6:10 PM

I decide to do some writing.

Part 2: The Blogger Lifestyle

Doing my 1000 words a day – or ideally 2000 – is something I usually don't manage while I'm travelling.

But today I've done it: blog post in the morning, email to my subscribers, and now this day in the life.

Why a day in the life?

Because sleepy as I am, it's easier than doing some serious travel writing. A better writer would pull some brilliant essay out of thin air.

Oh well. Maybe I'll be brilliant tomorrow. After some more sleep.

6:52 PM

Hurtling through the air towards an unknown future in a foreign country.

The pilot comes back on to announce we're flying over Santander. One of my favorite Spanish cities.

In a couple of hours I'll be home. My sofa. My bed. My wall of books. My windows on Madrid's skyline.

What am I doing with my life, anyway?

I'm still not sure. So I just try to focus on processes.

Write those 2000 words a day.

Do pushups. Drink water. And wine.

Sleep 8 hours when I can.

Eat meat, fish and vegetables.

Publish. Sell. Market. Edit.

Videos. Ebooks. Photos. Articles.

Did Hemingway have a life plan? Win the Nobel and then blow your brains out?

Note to self: don't idolize Hemingway.

Part 2: The Blogger Lifestyle

7:02 PM

Went back and edited. Still have no idea where this article – or my life – is going. It seems like there must be a logical conclusion to all this somewhere.

In the meantime, I'm speeding through the air in a metal and glass tube, somewhere over Castile.

The pilot comes back on the PA.

"So hey guys, we're just getting a bit of turbulence up here…"

Half an hour later I'm on the ground.

And soon after, back at my foreign home.

Part 2: The Blogger Lifestyle

High Quality Problems

If there's one thing I've learned since firing my boss, it's this: having your own business is hard.

But I've already talked about that.

So if there are two things, the second one is that you've really, really, REALLY gotta practice gratitude.

Because my high quality blogger-life problems are other people's biggest life dreams.

It doesn't always feel like it at the time... and that's why I have to remind myself.

For example: sometimes I have to visit my accountant on Gran Vía to learn about international tax laws so I can avoid being completely screwed by one government or another.

It's not much fun, it costs lots of money, and it feels like a huge time suck.

But then I think, "Wait... it's a Thursday afternoon and most of my friends are at work – probably teaching classes till 9:30pm. Meanwhile, I'm taking a leisurely stroll down Gran Vía to see my accountant...

"Because motherfucker, I ain't broke no more!"

When I was younger, I honestly never thought I'd be the kind of guy who has adult-type plans for his day like going to see an accountant.

I figured by this point in my life I'd probably be spending my Thursday afternoons cooking meth in my kitchen, or selling plasma to make the rent payment.

I was wrong. And it's glorious.

Part 2: The Blogger Lifestyle

Here's another one: sometimes I'm in a nice place (AirBnB in Budapest, hotel in the Canary Islands, wherever) and I'm pretty disappointed that the WiFi just sucks.

At which point I have to get up, take my laptop, and find a better hotel. A hotel with a better Wifi connection, where I can sit in their lobby and do my 3-hour work day while drinking overpriced beer and watching fashionable people on vacation walk by.

It's actually pretty sweet. Bad WiFi and all.

Anyway, what I'm trying to say here: if you don't appreciate what you have now, you won't appreciate it later when you have more.

So appreciate it all.

Appreciate the struggle. Appreciate the pain. Appreciate the joy.

As Tyler Durden said in *Fight Club*: This is your life, and it's ending, one minute at a time.

So just go out and enjoy it. Every vanishing minute.

Do it for me. Or do it for you. But just do it.

Thanks for reading, and thanks for everything.

Always your biggest fan,

Daniel.

Madrid, Spain, June 2017.

Part 2: The Blogger Lifestyle

Epilogue

I'm writing this final chapter on another fast train, this time to Valencia.

Hurtling across Spanish countryside at 230 km/h, olive trees and grape vines whizzing past outside the window.

Here I am.

The two year mark has come and gone – more than two years since I fired my boss and walked away to live the life I had always wanted.

And that's why I'm able to pick up on a random Thursday morning, with little notice, to head to the beach.

But enough about me...

Here's something I haven't mentioned directly, but it's maybe the most important thing of all.

If there's one thing I've learned in this 7-year journey, it's this:

You've gotta give to others.

And you've gotta be useful.

Do something for the rest of humanity, no matter how small... because that's how humanity moves forward. Little by little.

If you can figure out a way to give more to more people, all your own problems will work themselves out.

I have no idea where I learned that, all those years ago. Maybe a marketing podcast, maybe some other blogger. I certainly wouldn't have come up with it on my own.

Either way, I remember my 29th birthday. I was in a park in the south of Madrid, where I had climbed a hill to contemplate the view, and to contemplate my life. I had a few hours before work.

Part 2: The Blogger Lifestyle

I'd just had a stroke of good luck that was so ridiculous and huge and improbable that I realized, suddenly, that karma does exist.

Maybe not in some literal Hindu sense.

But karma.

It's a real thing. And I decided that day to make giving to others one of my main life goals.

Because somehow, it always comes back.

And guess what?

The power of blogging had played a large part in this huge stroke of luck.

I realized this, and felt transformed. I felt like I had a new perspective on life, all of the sudden.

I was probably making about 10 bucks a week back then, off of Google ads. Hardly even a supplement to my teaching income. But I decided that if I could figure out a way to help a million people to learn English, I'd certainly be able to make a living off it.

Somehow.

It took me years to actually figure out the how. But giving and adding value is something you can start today.

Start before you're ready.

Start now.

And feel free to write me to tell me how it goes.

I'm here: expatmadrid.com/contact

And by the way...

••••

I really hope you enjoyed the book. For much more awesomeness about blogging, new articles, and more, head to expatmadrid.com/book

And if you're feeling kind, please take a few minutes to leave a review on Amazon. It really helps get the word out.

Thanks!

Thank You

• • • •

Really, I'd like to thank everybody.

Because you can learn from every situation. And every person.

More specifically, I'd like to thank Anthony Metivier of magneticmemorymethod.com (for all the great advice and inspiration that helped me go full time as a blogger), Gloria Atanmo of theblogabroad.com (for her incredible honesty and transparency, which I admire endlessly), Jane (who told me I needed to write this book so often that I finally listened) and Stuart (for pointing out my own bullshit).

And to all my online mentors who I've never met but I hope to someday kick it with – in Madrid or elsewhere: Joe Polish and Dean Jackson, Ramit Sethi, Tim Ferriss, Steven Pressfield, and many more.

Plus all my friends, lovers, teachers, ex-bosses and ex-girlfriends for putting up with me and my insane ambitions… no matter how briefly.

Thanks y'all… love ya.

Daniel Welsch.

Madrid, Spain.

July 2017.

www.ingramcontent.com/pod-product-compliance
Lightning Source LLC
Chambersburg PA
CBHW070258230526
45470CB00002B/632